OPEN DOORS

Bristol's hidden interiors

Stephen Morris
Tim Mowl

redcliffe

First published in 2002 by Redcliffe Press Ltd.,
81g Pembroke Road, Bristol BS8 3EA
Telephone: 0117 973 7207

ISBN 1 900178 59 1
British Library Cataloguing-in-Publication Data.
A catalogue record for this book is available from the British Library.

Designed and typeset by Stephen Morris Communications, smc@freeuk.com, Bristol and Liverpool,
and printed by HSW Printers, Tonypandy, Rhondda.

Acknowledgments

The photographs in this book exist because so many people responded enthusiastically to my requests for access. Individuals
are too numerous to mention, but I am especially indebted to the Bristol Museums Service, Bristol City Council, the Trust of
the New Room ('John Wesley's Chapel'), and to Compact Power.
My special thanks go to the people who allowed their homes to be photographed.
Dedicated to Graham, Raymond and Pat.

Stephen Morris. Bristol, August 2002.

Introduction

'I've passed the building on the bus many times and have always been curious about it'

This comment, just one of the many we receive every year, helps to explain why Bristol Doors Open Day is such a success. For one day each year places of architectural or historic interest, not usually accessible, or fully accessible, to the general public, open up their doors; and each year on that second Saturday in September up to 50,000 visits are recorded.

The appeal is wide: last year we found, in a small sample, visitors from every Bristol postal district, as well as Bath, Wells, Taunton, Exeter, Cambridge, London, New Zealand, USA and Russia.

In 1994 the first 28 Bristol buildings opened their doors; in 2002 we have our 100th building. All are examples in different ways of Bristol's fine and varied architecture, both contemporary and historic. We were one of the first English cities to hold such an event, and today no other city outside London has more venues or more visitors.

And no other city has its own souvenir book! This record of around half the venues, past and present – with Tim's inimitable, lively and well-informed text and Stephen's striking photographs – is a splendid celebration of this popular event.

Thanks to them both; and to the many owners, to the multitude of helpers on the Day and to the organising committee, all of whose hard work makes the event possible; to the sponsors who have kindly provided financial support and to those who each year help in kind; and to the Bristol Chamber of Commerce & Initiative, partners in its initiation and who now underwrite us. Without the help and enthusiasm of these supporters there would be no Bristol Doors Open Day for all of us to enjoy.

Finally, and most importantly, thank you to the thousands of visitors to these wonderful buildings, the Day is dedicated to you.

Penny Mellor
Organiser, Bristol Doors Open Day.

Bristol Doors Open Day is organised in partnership by the Bristol Architecture Centre, the Bristol Chamber of Commerce & Initiative and Bristol City Council. Nationally, it is a part of the Heritage Open Days co-ordinated by the Civic Trust.

Bristol Royal Hospital for Children, Upper Maudlin Street

The new Children's Hospital, designed by David Radford of Whicheloe Macfarlane MDP, and officially opened by the Prince of Wales on 2 July 2001, did not have to be a very good building to outpoint its near neighbours. Immediately above it up the hill is the Brutalist Oncology Centre that seems to have been designed to terrify any unfortunate cancer patient entering its levels of artificially soot-stained concrete; while next to it is that strange extension to Percy Adams and Charles Holden's original 1906-11 hospital which conceals most of the fine Edwardian detail, has neither horizontal nor vertical drive, no central feature and only a depressing heap of grey concrete spillikins dividing its irregular fenestration.

Radford's new hospital, with 169 beds, most of them with a parent's bed alongside, garden courtyards and lavish play facilities, is at least cheerful and brightly coloured. It climbs the hill with a pleasant irregularity, almost Art Deco in its insistence on flat roofs and big angle windows. It would be perfectly at home functioning as a holiday hotel overlooking the Pacific beaches of California rather than Upper Maudlin Street. An interior emphasis on cheerfulness that pervades its art and decoration begins at the entrance with a huge immobile lollipop mobile. Every effort has been made to 'create a relaxed and interesting environment' and to 'reduce fear and tension for the child and for the family'. Children, however, grow up fast and it would be interesting to know how the nine-year-olds react to a décor that appears aimed at three to seven-year-olds. Do children want adult interpretations of child art or adult art aimed at children? Do they enjoy being condescended to with simple outlines and colours?

The fund raising campaign, spearheaded by Aardman's Wallace and Gromit's Grand Appeal, raised £12 million of which £1 million was used by arts co-ordinator Lesley Greene to bring together the work of over twenty artists to create the interior. At Reception there is a clock from which every fourteen minutes a monkey pops out and blows bubbles. On Level 2 (each level is colour-coded so that children can find their own way around) there is a Dolphin Clock by Kit Williams, music by Terry Oldfield.

A Playroom Corridor on Level 5 has Frank Egerton's relief interactive work, courtesy of SWEB. There is Roger Michell's poetry by Mike Hughes at the Hydrotherapy Pool, Sonja Andrews' banners in the Courtyard and the promise that there will be an Artist in Residence near the Play Centre. Radio Lollipop broadcasts from the Play Centre Studio in the evenings and at weekends, and the goodwill that has been poured into the premises is awesome. The problem, one suspects, will be persuading the children to quit the place when they are better.

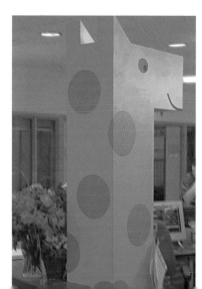

The Wesley House, 4 Charles Street

If Bristol still has a lingering Low Church, evangelical and non-conformist religious profile then Charles Wesley's twenty-one year sojourn (1749-71) in this red brick, step-voussoired house, cramped between ill-mannered commercial premises in Charles Street, may have something to do with it. Marriage suited Charles just as much as it frustrated and bored his brother John. Charles was probably the better preacher of the two brothers, but John was the organiser of the Methodists, and whereas John loved to travel and encourage the brethren, not only in Britain but in America, Charles was never happier than when he was writing hymns in this little house with his wife Sarah, or 'Sally', the daughter of a prosperous mid-Wales squire, Marmaduke Gwynne.

She was nineteen years younger than Charles and, before her mother would give permission for the match, Charles had to give assurances of a steady income of £100 a year from his hymn writing. But Sally settled happily in this simple house with its little fruit garden at the back. Nine children were born to them here; three of them – Charles junior in 1757, Sally junior in 1759 and Samuel the musician in 1766 – survived to adulthood. They were all baptised at St James's church where the baptismal register records them as the children of 'Charles & of Sarah a Precher in the Horsfaier'.

Life in 4 Charles Street was not always easy. Charles was a vegetarian and something of a crank. He considered raw fruit to be a poison and wrote home once to his wife saying: 'If you cannot keep Sally from eating poison, I must grub up all the trees in the garden or take another house without one. Give my love to Charles. I know not what to say to Sally unless she has quite given up eating raw fruit. Then you may give my love to her also.'

In 1753 Mrs Wesley almost died here of confluent smallpox. That destroyed her looks, so that the near twenty-year disparity in their ages was no longer marked. Charles, however, told her that in his eyes she was as fair as ever. Sadly little Jacky Wesley caught the same sickness and did not survive. 'I shall go to him,' his mother wrote, 'but he shall never return to me.' Jacky had been a musical prodigy, and Samuel would follow later with the same precocious talents. It was to educate him that the family decided to move to London. Their Bristol house had always been rented and they had been offered a house of their own in Chesterfield Street, Marylebone, with a twenty-year lease still to run and a well stocked wine cellar. With that inducement Charles Wesley left Bristol for ever and the house where six of his children had died and where he had written, among other hymns, 'Jesu lover of my soul'. Savour its brooding simplicities and its atmosphere of bourgeois homeliness faithfully preserved.

St James's Priory, Whitson Street

St James's Priory church has Bristol's oldest interior. The Earl of Gloucester founded the Priory in 1129, which makes it twenty or even forty years earlier than the Norman chapter house in the cathedral. But whereas that is a rather magisterial interior space, the nave of St James, which is all that has survived of a larger building, has a pleasantly ramshackle, down-at-heel look, representing the accidents of several centuries on a Norman base. The polished Aberdeen granite Gothic work in the north aisle dates from 1864, executed with the Victorians' usual ill-founded self-confidence.

To make matters more complicated there is almost as much neo-Norman work of the mid-nineteenth century as there is genuine Norman building of the twelfth century. Stephen Morris was drawn to the crisp, well preserved neo-Norman more than to the genuine article and he has, accordingly, taken the pulpit and east end wall, on both of which round arches intersect to make a prophecy of the next style to come, the pointed arched Early English Gothic. That was the kind of erudite detail which Victorian fans of the neo-Norman relished. Nikolaus Pevsner, however, hated the style, which he saw as a feeble and clumsy English version of his native German Italianate-Rundbogenstil. That distaste explains the frigid tone and grudging detail of his account of St James, which is surely one of the city's most likeable churches, in his 1958 North Somerset and Bristol volume of the *Buildings of England* series.

The west front has an astonishing survival, a beautiful wheel window from the first building period, with a rope carving running around eight small circles about a large inner circle. Its design is ingenious and its survival up there exposed to the weather is remarkable, but Pevsner can only describe it as 'extremely odd'. Inside there is nothing half as sophisticated, but St James has all the air of a much loved village church such as the artist and topographer John Buckler used to draw in the pre-restoration days of the early nineteenth century. The Church of England could think of nothing to do with this ancient holy place, but at least the Bishop had the grace to lend it on virtually permanent lease to a Roman Catholic order which makes a speciality of care for the homeless and the drug-afflicted in the inner cities. They have not only brought St James back to life again, with regular offices and the Sacrament reserved, but they have made an attractive enclosure of its forecourt by constructing, in roughly 1690s pastiche, a residential block for the Brothers and those they look after. The tower of the church is said to be a seventeenth- and nineteenth-century composite, but if that is so then whoever designed it had in mind the thirteenth- and fourteenth-century tower of St Thomas of Canterbury at Pucklechurch where the tower is a dead ringer for St James.

Wesley's New Room, Horsefair

George Whitfield preached out in the fields of Kingswood to a crowd of miners on 13 February 1739. Shocked by their near-pagan savagery he called John Wesley in to help him in Bristol, and on 2 April that year Wesley preached from a stone on a hillock at Baptist Mills, following up with more sermons in Nicholas Street, Castle Street and Gloucester Street. Winning large numbers of converts but still excluded by the clergy from Bristol's churches, the two men determined to build the first chapel for their orderly 'methodical' version of Christianity, and on 12 May 1739 the foundation stone for the 'New Room' was laid. Significantly, it was sited in Broadmead among prosperous merchant premises, not out in the rough coalfields of Kingswood.

The Quaker builder George Tully, who is known to have designed the Friends' Meeting House at Quakers Friars a year later, was almost certainly the designer of this new chapel. As first built, deliberately hidden away from the streets, its interior was like some large garden building, a square hall lit by an octagonal dome supported on four stone Tuscan columns. There were two floors of accommodation for the minister and his family up above the hall and looking down into it. A double-decker pulpit takes the place and the focus point of an altar, but a railed enclosure still recalls Anglican communion rails. In 1748 the New Room was extended and two more columns were added.

To finance this simple geometry and order, within a potentially chaotic and enclosed space, the Methodists devised their contribution toll of a penny a week from all converts: an ordered finance for ordered woodwork. Walk from this essential Protestantism to the Catholic exuberance of the choir vaults at Bristol Cathedral and it hardly seems possible that the same human impulses were working to create such different places for worship of the same God.

Eighteen Methodist conferences were held here in Wesley's lifetime, the first of them on 1 August 1745; and it was at the 1771 conference that Wesley famously refused to alter his stance on 'free grace', which so greatly modified and softened the severe Calvinistic doctrine of pre-destination. Captain Webb of the 48th regiment of foot, one of the founders of Methodism in America, was converted here by a Wesley sermon, and Charles Wesley wrote many of his hymns in Bristol. It was here too that John, his brother, ordained Coke as a bishop and Whatcoat and Vasey as presbyters to go out to serve Methodism in the USA in what would inevitably become a body separate from the Church of England to which Wesley himself still belonged.

Smiles' Brewery, Upper Maudlin Street

Smiles' Brewery stands appropriately on that rough and sturdy brick revetment, a rarely noticed triumph of late-Georgian engineering, behind Johnny Ball Lane off Lewin's Mead, which holds up a whole street of shops, houses and small manufactories below Park Row. If Johnny Ball Lane or, for that matter, Zed Alley, are unknown thoroughfares to you, hunt them out on the way to the brewery and experience Dickensian Bristol almost in the raw. It seems appropriate too that Smiles, perched precariously up there, should use basic gravity to manufacture beers.

Built on a vertical tower structure it stores malt and hops on the top floor with tanks of hard Bristol water. These raw materials drop down to the brewing floor. In the mash tuns, one of which can be seen in the window on Upper Maudlin Street, the roasted malted barley and fermentable sugars get to work on that hard water, producing a liquid wort which is then introduced to the bitter hops and finally to Smiles' very own strain of yeast. After a week of these processes the young green beer goes down again to the casks to mature.

The result is a beer that, though many women like it, can fairly be described as masculine and uncompromising, the Platonic essence, it is not too much to say, of a strong English beer, and the absolute opposite of lager. That is exactly what the Smiles directors set out to produce in the effete 1970s when thin, pale drink was sweeping the market. They began merely producing enough beer for one restaurant then went into full scale brewing in 1978. Since then their brew, which they like to describe as 'subtle and enigmatic', has gained favour and sold throughout Britain.

In case the shiny machinery in the illustration looks disturbingly high-tech, rest easy, it is only a cask washer on the bottom floor next to the racking tanks. After your Open Doors visit make sure you drop into Smiles' Brewery Tap, which has the best modern interior in any Bristol pub.

Foster's Almshouses Chapel, Colston Street

In 1481 John Foster founded this almshouse with its chapel dedicated to the Three Kings of Cologne, and in 1882 John Foster rebuilt the Almshouse and virtually rebuilt, though the polite word is 'refaced', the Chapel. And no, this is not a case of a Bristol rival to Methuselah; they were two quite separate and apparently unrelated John Fosters. The first Foster was Mayor of the city in that year, so the Chapel was a devout celebration of his worldly success. He was a merchant trading, among other commodities, in salt with the Rhineland, where he may have developed a devotion to the great Gothic church, dedicated to the Three Kings, in Cologne. Their relics were brought from Milan to Cologne in 1164. The 'Kings' had originally been the three Magi, priests of an obscure Persian sect, who had visited the infant Christ in Bethlehem; but the Middle Ages liked to take a feudal, hierarchical slant on events and the Magi had become kings representing the black, brown and white races making homage to the Almighty. There is no other church or chapel of the period dedicated to them in this country.

That first John Foster was one of Bristol's two MPs in 1489; in 1492 he died leaving endowments for one priest and thirteen poor persons in his foundation. There was a rebuilding programme in 1708 when the Chapel was classicised. So when in 1861 the second John Foster, of the busy architectural practice of Foster and Wood, came to a second rebuilding and extension of the accommodation for twenty-four additional residents, there was not much of the original medieval chapel left to restore except its first dimensions. Foster's work on the Almshouse in French Burgundian style went on for more than twenty years. He gave the little Chapel its rock-faced entrance front, built its complex substructure of shops and re-carved its resting niches on Christmas Steps.

In a further bout of restoration in 1962 Ernest Pascoe, a Bristol craftsman, carved the statues of the Three Kings over the doorway and an Irishman, Patrick Pollen, designed the glass for the striking window over the altar. This, with its harsh, dramatic leading is typical of a post-war mood of brutalism in stained glass for churches. The baby Jesus is represented as symbolically crucified on his mother's lap.

The only truly old feature of the Chapel is Sir John Duddlestone's candelabrum, gifted in 1696, but its interior has a charming intimacy and immediacy. When there is a full congregation and Communion is being celebrated the chalice has to be passed from hand to hand rather than administered directly by the priest.

Unitarian Meeting House, Lewin's Mead

The Unitarians of Bristol in the eighteenth century made up a very wealthy group of worshippers, and they were also, in keeping with their interpretation of the Godhead, up-to-date, logical and direct. This explains the structure of the Meeting House which they commissioned a London-trained surveyor and architect, William Blackburn, to design for them in 1787 and which was built between 1788 and 1791. In 1782 Blackburn won a competition to erect prisons under the Penitentiary Act of 1779. Blackburn was a prison architect who built or altered seventeen gaols in his short (1750-90) lifetime. He designed the County Bridewell in Lawford's Gate, Bristol in 1787 and when he died at Preston he was on his way to Glasgow to design his eighteenth house of correction. For his times Blackburn was a modernist architect and a strict functionalist who pioneered radial design in prison layouts. He was a supporter and intimate of the great prison reformer, John Howard, and his functional planning could well have been what attracted the Unitarians to him. With a Spanish mother and a father who was a tradesman in Southwark, he had none of the usual gentlemanly or traditionalist hang-ups of his profession. An inspection of the side walls of the Meeting House will reveal shades of his prison-house practice in the austerity of the elevations, the lack of relieving mouldings and ornament in the two great tripartite windows.

To face the carriage entrance and the road, however, there is a suave Robert Adam handling to the Chapel's elegantly assured principal façade. Michael Jenner makes a subtle criticism of Blackburn's handling, suggesting that the joints of the rustication are too shallow to convey the required masculine solidity for the base of the building, while the windows are set too far forward in their recesses, rendering the composition two-dimensional. Visitors can make their own judgements. Inside the situation is naturally reversed because the window sills are satisfyingly deep and the walls need to look solid to support the tremendous span of the heavily coffered roof, which covers a seventy-foot wide by forty-foot deep space without a single arch or column. The secret to Blackburn's conjuring trick is apparently that the ceiling is suspended on chains from the hidden timber roof trusses, but the effect, with the huge windows, is one of light and airy freedom with a complete absence of mystery. Lightly poised galleries run around three sides of this space; the slim pulpit and its approach stairs have survived the conversion of it all into office premises, but the box pews that once brought the sight lines down have all gone, replaced now by modern desks and computer terminals, except for a few around the entrance. Perched on the terraced escarpment behind the Chapel is the even more austere School Room of 1824-6: faith and aesthetics in perfect accord.

St John-on-the-Wall, Broad Street

Guarded, not by two saints, but by twin giants, and with two entirely different churches set one above the other, St John-on-the-Wall is anything but an ordinary ecclesiastical building, more an enchantingly dusty and unexpected compendium of Bristol's history, surviving improbably among modern office blocks. The giants, Brennus and Belinus, were the mythical founders of the city and the rich merchant, Walter Frampton, who built St John's somewhere in the middle of the fourteenth century (he died in 1388), has his coat of arms set next to those of the city between these favoured local giants. His tomb is inside the Upper Church on the left of the altar. The tower of the church is set over the old Frome Gate which once led out from the inner or Norman walls of Bristol; the slot for its portcullis is still visible. A livelier relic, recently restored by the City Council, is St John's Conduit, splashing away on the north wall of the church enough water to have supplied a quarter of the old medieval city. Drinking is not recommended because the water has come down through 600-year old lead pipes and pierced elm logs from the spring up on Brandon Hill and some historians claim that lead poisoning destroyed the Roman empire.

The Lower Church or Crypt is at its best when the afternoon sun is pouring in to light up the low vaulted interior. It was a Chapel of the Holy Cross, a guild fraternity and its eastern half is just on the stylistic cusp between Decorated and Perpendicular Gothic; it is more curvaceous than the angular, purely Perpendicular western half. Look out for Green Men in the leaf carvings of the vault bosses, two holy water stoops and a beautiful ogee-headed tomb recess.

In the Upper Church there is much more to see: Walter Frampton's tomb, Minton tiles in the sanctuary, a Caroline communion table of 1635 and, slightly later, more sophisticated communion rails, a Georgian sword rest and, best of all, Thomas Rowley's 1478 brass. This may have been what inspired 'the marvellous boy', Thomas Chatterton, a tragic, short-lived mid-eighteenth-century poet, to invent a fifteenth-century poet monk called Thomas Rowley and to fake Rowley's medieval poetry. For a few years Chatterton deceived everyone, but his clumsy forgeries were revealed, he was rejected and he committed suicide by poisoning. Some of the woodwork in the gallery at the west end of the Upper Church is almost as suspect as Rowley's poetry. An 1828 restoration made a confusion here when it blocked the original west door.

It is strange that two buildings so characterfully and intensely Bristolian cannot find a use in the modern city. Perhaps St James's Priory points a way in its new role.

At present St John's is under the care of the Churches Conservation Trust and regularly open during the week with a charming volunteer, Hugo, on hand to explain its history and open the Crypt.

Christ Church, Broad Street

Friends of St Mary Redcliffe might not agree, but Christ Church has, after the choir of the cathedral, the most numinous and exhilarating religious interior in Bristol. To walk through its low, dark vestibule into the airy complexity of its nave catches the breath with surprise. Six emaciated columns strain up on tip-toe with those illogical chunks of entablature balanced on their acanthus capitals, and the shallow saucer vaults on top of them seem not so much supported as tethered down to stop them floating away. An English church is usually so predictable: a west to east progression of arches, a long corridor with big windows and a dark roof. Christ Church, in contrast, is a unity of Mozartian cheerfulness, a spatial whole of cream and gold to be absorbed entire at the instant of entry. It works like a confident cantata to a humane but probably quite intellectual Creator.

Young William Paty designed this space in 1786 when he was brimming with ideas soon after completing his architectural training in London. Those columns and the saucer domes are modelled, not on the ducal church at Badminton, which is often cited as his inspiration, but on Sir Robert Taylor's Transfer Offices (now demolished) in the Bank of England. Taylor was the architect who came closest to propelling our staid and rule-bound Palladian style into the more bucolic continental Rococo, and there are Rococo touches all over Christ Church. The leading lay parishioner of the church was old Thomas Tyndall who had added, back in the late 1750s, superb Rococo interiors to his house, the Royal Fort. Garlands of flowers twine around the columns of the Eating Room door-case at the Royal Fort. The same garlands twine around the columns of what was originally the reredos at Christ Church, but which was re-erected in 1928 as a choir screen after a nineteenth-century vicar had replaced it in 1883 with the present ponderous stone reredos. Look carefully at the six columns of the nave and just the ghost of painted garlands, that once were twined around them, can be distinguished: more Rococo touches. As for the cherubs on the pulpit above the emblems of the Passion, they are by the Paty carvers at their best and would grace any church in Vienna. The beautiful neo-Classical altar table must also be from the Paty workshop. Faded copies of Italian masterpieces hang on the walls, enhancing the un-English atmosphere, but Sunday Evensong here is a time-trip back into the age of Dickens. The organ, a Renatus Harris, in a case dating in parts from about 1700, is older than the church. Opinions vary as to its tone because it was built for the much larger spaces of the medieval Christ Church.

Old Council House, Corn Street

When high-minded councillors or self-important lawyers demand spacious new premises with all mod cons they often leave buildings that were architecturally superior to their new homes, empty and functionless. Bristol's handsome Old Council House in Corn Street still lies locked and lonely except on Open Doors days years after it was proposed as a venue for civic marriages.

Sir Robert Smirke, who prepared plans for it in 1822 and had it built by 1827, made a special line for himself in county halls. Bristol's was one of eight that he designed, Carlisle, Gloucester, Hereford, Lincoln, Maidstone, Perth and Shrewsbury being the others. Two local Bristol architects, Thomas and James Foster, admired his design of the Ionic columns in antis so much that they copied them for their Upper and Lower Arcades in Broadmead even before the Council had got round to building Smirke's proposals. Quite why the street façade of the Council House stumbles so irregularly no one has ever explained, but it was much mocked at the time: 'Why yonder Mansion stands awry,/Does Bristol wondering seek -/Like to its Councils is its Site,/Oblique – Oblique – Oblique!' The new building replaced the old Council House and St Ewen's Church sited on the corner of Corn Street and Broad Street.

If it was Smirke's fault he made up for it by his sumptuously polychromatic Council Chamber interior, all gilt and coffering and unexpected terracotta shades, a true Regency colour scheme, subtly top lit by that beautiful lantern. Only the decorative stencil work on the walls is later. Even the treads of the grand staircase are polychromatic with their brass inlay on a dark red composition. Smirke meant his British Museum in London to be highly coloured like this, not drab and stone coloured.

The big Court Room behind the Council Chamber is later and it is here that a generally disregarded set of splendid historical paintings hang. They should all be in our City Museum & Art Gallery, but these days it is almost an artistic sin to admire a figurative composition. Take a chance to wallow in that aesthetic vice here. The best known is *Mistress Dorothy Hazard and the women of Bristol defending the Frome Gate against Prince Rupert* in the Civil War, but there is a Frank Brangwyn of the *Chairing of Edmund Burke*, and John Hassall's *State entry of Queen Elizabeth into the city in 1574*, where she looks very like the Queen as played in the *Blackadder* series on TV. She came in through Lawford's Gate at the end of Old Market and the mayor presented her with a hundred pounds in gold pieces. The pageant they staged for her lasted four days with much gunpowder and storming of fortresses.

As you leave it is worth noticing the difference between Smirke's suave handling of his Greek Revival material and the raw, correct scholarship, half-digested, of the western extension to the Corn Street front by Richard Shackleton Pope, added in 1829 to supply a Magistrate's Court. Finally, look up at E H Baily's figure of Justice who is armed with a sword but was never given her balance!

Lloyds TSB Bank, Corn Street

Where else but in mercantile, philistine Bristol would you find a bank that was much more beautiful than the two eighteenth-century churches on the other side of the road? This has to be one of Bristol's top ten buildings, the brightest star in a street with at least twelve other buildings of real quality, our not entirely unworthy rival to the Grand Canal in Venice or the Golden Street in Genoa. It is kind of Lloyds to put their palazzo on the Open Doors list, but to be perfectly honest the exterior is ten times more exciting than the banking hall inside.

There are reasons for that falling off. The exterior, or the right-hand five bays of it, was designed in 1854 by the city's nineteenth-century unpredictable – William Bruce Gingell – with some help from his partner, William Royce Lysaght, and it went up between 1854 and 1858 as the prestige base of the West of England and South Wales Bank. It was bought by Lloyds in 1892 and that was when a sixth bay was added at the entrance side. Now that it has all been superbly manicured and cleaned, and delicately veiled in a fine mesh of almost invisible wire to discourage the starlings, it is easy to tell which bay is the later Edwardian fake because there is a double column on the upper floor to mark the junction and the new bay is all grey Portland stone, lacking the contrast of rich golden Bath stone in the earlier Victorian work.

Gingell's model was Jacopo Sansovino's Biblioteca Marciana in the Piazza San Marco, Venice but, unusually for such derivative work, the bank is richer, more three-dimensional than the Library. Catch it on some February afternoon when the sun slants diagonally across it and the contrasts and inventions would be enough to make John Ruskin, of *Stones of Venice* fame, if he were still alive, swoon with pleasure that the cold English could design with such warm hearts. The sculpture is always attributed to John Evan Thomas, a Gloucestershire-born sculptor who was working at the time on the new Houses of Parliament. But it was carved by his workmen to his direction. It includes carved compliments to Bristol, Bath, Exeter, Newport, Cardiff and four English and Welsh rivers. The hyperactive cherubs on the frieze are busy symbolising Justice, Integrity, Education, Charity, Peace, Plenty, Art, Science, Navigation and Commerce: Victorian cherubs were not allowed to hang around idly on tombstones.

The banking hall inside is just a little of a disappointment, but it was substantially reworked in the standard handsome English classicism of Lloyds' house style. The roof replaces Gingell's lavish vault with its twelve skylights, but the coupled Corinthian columns round the walls are Gingellian survivals. On the month when it opened in 1856 *The Builder* remarked sourly that 'if any architectural attraction could reconcile a man to any rate of discount, no customer should ever go away dissatisfied'.

The Exchange, Corn Street

The building of the Exchange began when the City Corporation sent a mission to treat with Ralph Allen at Bath on 19 December 1740 and ended with a ceremonial opening on 21 September 1743. By bringing in John Wood the Elder of Bath as its architect and Allen's workforce for the fine, as opposed to the rough, masonry Bristol had reluctantly admitted that its rival sister city was far in advance in the stylistic handling of Palladian design and the application of a smooth ashlar finish to façades. Where Bristol craftsmen were superior was in carving Bath stone into fantastic decorative detail. Wood's Exchange has, in its frieze and around its inner courtyard, far more ornamental carving than was usual on a chastely austere Palladian building. Thomas Paty, of the long established Bristol firm of Patys, father and sons, supplied the enrichments which make a close study of the Exchange so rewarding.

Records preserved in the Royal Academy's Library in London reveal that those two-and-a-half building years were stormy. Bristol Corporation set up Captain Edward Foy as clerk of works to report on Wood for malpractice. Foy was so hostile that Wood had to employ a second clerk of works, David Lewis, on a larger salary, in order to get anything done. Bath masons reported that they lived in dread of threats from the Bristol rough masons, who claimed in turn that they were underpaid. Wood was desperate to be allowed to make the open, single-storeyed courtyard behind the Exchange into a two-storey 'Egyptian Hall'. He had to be content with the existing Corinthian single-storey loggia, but the courtyard was eventually given a further storey with a rich ornamental roof by Edward Middleton Barry in 1872. This was removed and a shallower roof inserted in 1949. Underneath the loggia are Paty's carvings of the three continents over the entrances: Europe,

Asia and Africa. There are Indian heads, penguins holding fish, crocodiles, gryphons and camels, while the palatial façade of the Exchange itself has elephants, rum barrels, bales and pineapples to symbolize the city's trading empire.

Behind that show front on the right of the entrance arch was a tavern and on the left a coffee house, both superior places where merchants could meet and discuss their deals. Goods would be exposed in the open courtyard to the back and bargains would be struck on the nails outside.

The complete building cost, including the land, was £56,352; Wood was paid a commission of £833. To celebrate, since his name was not mentioned in the Mayor's opening speech, Wood published a poem in a broadsheet: 'Such art Palladio – and such Jones – was thine!/And such is Wood's – who rear'd this spacious Dome/A finish'd Wonder for each Age to come'. His real recognition came when Liverpool, Bristol's trading rival, promptly commissioned him to build a similar grand exchange for them with the crowning dome that Wood had wanted to build at Bristol.

Broadmead Baptist Church, Lower Union Street

This is 'the church over the shops', and very business-like and business-integrated it is. Anyone used to Anglican or Roman Catholic church premises will be intrigued and impressed by the modern face of Nonconformity in Bristol. The Baptists are a very old congregation in the city. The Rev. Haggard was preaching in St Ewen's in Corn Street back in the 1620s, when dissenters were stirring and the established Church of England was unsure of its own identity. As a separate community the Baptists took on their own premises, their Ebenezer, in 1640, becoming much stronger during the Civil War and the Commonwealth. There was a period of persecution under Charles II when the minister, the Rev. Hardcastle, was thrown into prison seven times between 1671 and 1678 for preaching and practising complete immersion.

After that, Bristol's Ebenezer settled down for almost three respectable centuries until the German blitz of 1940-41. The chapel was shaken by bombs, but not destroyed, and it was after the war that the whole functional value of one big chapel in addition to a big chapel hall was questioned. There could have been a move out into the suburbs, but Bristol's Baptists decided to stay where they had always been: with the city workers. Accordingly the nineteenth-century Ebenezer Chapel was pulled down and Ronald Simms designed the multi-purpose complex which now lies over Tesco on The Horsefair. It was opened in 1969 and has aimed, ever since, to be open between 9.30 am and 4.30 pm on weekdays for rest and contemplation when city workers feel that life is becoming overwhelming.

The general impression of the interior is cold and shadowy. A tall rectangle of grey concrete shoots up in the middle of the stairs and all the walls are in the same reserved colour; pale brown woodwork offers the only relief. There are rooms sprouting off from every landing of its three floors: the Hiley Room, the Marsham Room, the Knibb Room and the big Wardelow Room. These are all available for meetings and committees. People like Marks & Spencer's retirees or Alcoholics Anonymous use them, and there is an Undercroft, designed in the 1980s by Derrick Long, a dark room with sumptuous green armchairs.

Lastly there is the Chapel itself, like a great, grey cinema, with walls of vertical wooden slats, a purple carpet and, dominating it all, nine padded, cream-coloured chairs behind a table. To one side is a cross, broken and uneven in the post-Auschwitz tradition. Clearly this 600-seater space has proved dysfunctional and a half circle of screens cuts off a little area where 'City Prayers' and 'City Communion' are held. Six stained glass windows from the old Ebenezer Chapel offer a sequence of piety and ornament in this faintly chilling modernity. Experience it and then try St James's and Christ Church for the contrasting faces of Catholic and Anglican Christianity.

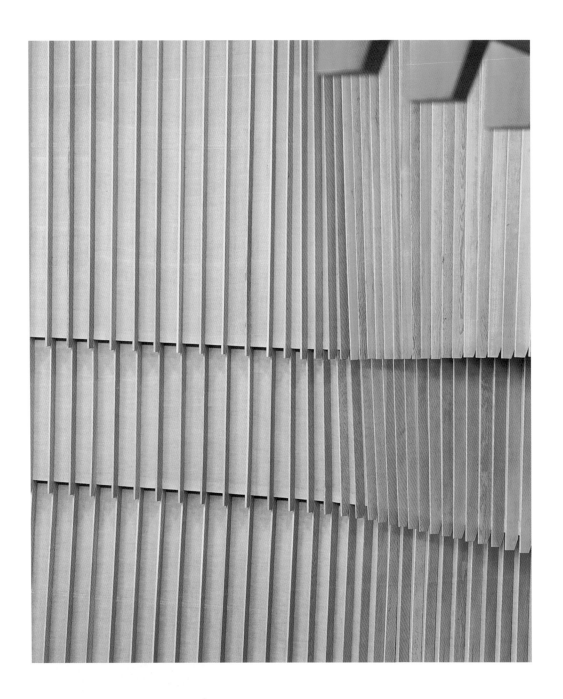

Theatre Royal, King Street

The Theatre Royal is both Bristol's pride and its problem. Thomas Paty built it between 1764 and 1766 to a design by the carpenter of London's Drury Lane Theatre, a Mr Sanderson, who was paid £38.16.8 for a plan of the interior, and it is the oldest theatre in the country to have been in virtually continual use since its opening: clearly a proud record. The problem is its seating capacity. This, by modern standards, is limited, making it hard to run at a profit. By those same standards it is, also, a museum piece and consequently inflexible. That horseshoe-shaped auditorium with its two tiers of circle boxes (the third tier was a later addition of 1800) may be photogenic, but many of the sight lines are interrupted by the supporting Doric columns. The eighteenth-century stage was brought forward two bays in the nineteenth century, resulting in a dramatic intimacy between audience and actors, but for modern producers that is not always enough. *She Stoops to Conquer* or a Noel Coward play projects splendidly, but the elegance of the décor, those Corinthian pilasters that frame the stage, inhibit anything savouring of the kitchen sink, gritty modern reality or even Strindberg intensities. Promenade productions and theatre in the round are, of course, impossible to stage.

In 1973 a compromise was attempted. Access to the theatre had always been unsatisfactory so the Coopers' Hall next door, a building of 1743-4 by William Halfpenny, was converted by the German émigré architect, Peter Moro, with much concrete, chromium trimming and purple carpeting, a style which he described as 'timeless', into a large foyer and bar for that interlude of drinks and social ritual without which theatres can rarely make ends meet. At the same time a new fly tower was constructed. Until then the backstage had been as much a museum piece as the front. Most of the original stage machinery of lifts and counter-balanced platforms had survived, but this had largely to be dismantled and stored.

Doubts are now being expressed about the wisdom of the Peter Moro conversion. Was the cavernous new space inside the Coopers' Hall wisely used? Do the 1970s fittings accord well with this eighteenth-century interior and its Georgian-style chandeliers? Instead of the low, cellar-like studio theatre, which Moro devised in the spaces of the old entrance from the street, could a sizeable second theatre be created elsewhere in the complex with the flexibility required for exciting innovations of production? Could such a new studio theatre be built on the roof, thereby freeing the entrance foyer to create a new space visually accessible from the street through a transparent wall? These are some of the exciting and innovative solutions that are being pursued by Moro's architectural firm, now led by Andrezj Blonski. With the help of a Heritage Lottery Fund grant the practice may soon be reshaping their founder's revamping, a mere thirty years after it was completed, to give the city an historic and an ultra-modern theatre on the same site.

Harvey's Wine Cellars, Denmark Street

An Open Doors Day visit to Harvey's Wine Museum in Denmark Street will not give entry to a wine and sherry tasting. For that you must join a private party of at least twenty, paying roughly £9 a head. What a free visit will give you is an experience of a hidden mercantile Bristol of dark cellars, a rare glimpse into the underground world that lies beneath most of the streets and premises of the old city. When he passed through Bristol in the 1730s on his way to the Hot Well, the poet Alexander Pope was shocked by the soot and stench and rowdy activity of England's second city, which he described as 'a dirty great shop'. In Denmark Street today that 'dirty great shop' can still be evoked visually, though not in sewerage smells or clattering porters' sledges. The rough grey warehouses still close in oppressively hiding out the weather, the few shops have a furtive air about them and taverns like The Hatchet are Long John Silver-worthy.

When William Perry founded his business on these premises in 1796 Bristol had passed its peak of prosperity as the slave trade moved to Liverpool. But it was still the hub of the wine trade with Spain and Portugal, the chief trading partner countries now that we were at war with France. Even so stocks of French brandy would still be holding out in those Bristol cellars as late as 1808. The essence of the trade was to buy cheap, to store long and to sell at a fat profit.

The cellars, which Perry bought and which Harvey's still occupy, date back to 1220 when they were dug under the Hospital, later the Priory, of St Mark, whose church survives as the Lord Mayor's Chapel. In 1806 the baker Thomas Urch joined William Perry in a shared capital enterprise of the already flourishing firm. When Urch's nephew, John Harvey, aged sixteen, was apprenticed to the firm in 1822, the Harvey connection, which still endures, had begun. John's father and grandfather had both been sea captains, but involved, Bristol fashion, in the three-cornered trade for West Indian sugar and rum. The firm's Royal Warrant was gained by John Harvey II in 1895. His grandson John (Jack) Harvey IV ran the firm until 1956, when successive takeovers by Showerings and Allied Domecq lost much of the family spirit, but a John Harvey V is still a director.

Sherry, Port and Madeira are not as fashionable as they were in the first two centuries of the firm. Wine is now the staple of business and these cellars have been converted into a carefully presented museum, complete with a period tavern restoration, long gloomy galleries and an excellent restaurant; hardly a time-trip, but still atmospheric.

St Mark's – The Lord Mayor's Chapel, College Green

If the Lord Mayor's Chapel and its contents were removed bodily to Florence or Siena it would become one of those churches to which tourists flock, pushing coins into slots to light sculpture and frescoes hidden away in dark corners. Because it is fixed solidly on College Green, entrance is free and they have to put a board out on the pavement inviting people in to enjoy its treasures. The Chapel is really a treasure house. Look down to the right as you come in and that kneeling marble figure of an eleven-year-old boy positively breathes quality. It is Caroline in date, of little John Cookin, who died in 1627, and it could easily be one of the rare surviving works of Nicholas Stone the elder, and one of his first. Next to it in a niche is a J M Rysbrack bust of Roman grandeur. It belongs on top of the monument next door, but they forgot to put it back after an exhibition. Opening behind it is the St Andrew's Chapel, so crammed with art that there is hardly room to walk. The strange black-and-white figure in the window over the entrance arch is St Thomas à Becket. William Beckford, the aesthete and collector of Fonthill Abbey, liked to believe that the saint was an ancestor and had the American artist, Benjamin West, design this for him in 1813. Someone should gild the ironwork screen; it is William Edney work of 1702 from the bombed Temple Church. Squeeze past the two prone Crusaders, Maurice de Gaunt and Robert de Gournay, menacing forms that Henry Moore would have appreciated, and there on the end wall, next to a squinch pointing at the high altar in the main Chapel, is a naïve sculptural masterpiece of 1667. Dame Mary Baynton is rising for the Resurrection Day as two soberly dressed Puritan angels pull back the curtains of mortality.

Back in the nave attention focuses on an equally naïve modern painting by Malcolm Ferguson behind the altar, its rigid figures and pastel colours command the eye, but do they then move the heart? Enjoy the ogee-arched tomb of Sir Maurice Berkeley on the left. It dates to 1465, but looks like a much richer 1310 design. Then dive down to the left, under the bad gumboil corbel, into the fan-vaulted, over restored Jesus, or Poyntz side chapel. It has the best medieval glass in the place, deep bold colours, and an entire floor of ugly but interesting sixteenth-century Spanish tiles. Those two arched niches on the left may be rare examples of medieval confessionals, offering sinners privacy.

On the way out in the nave, spare that splendid space a glance. It is a 1230 Early English Gothic try-out for that wall of glass, rectangular box formula, which will climax 300 years later in King's College Chapel, Cambridge: logical, English and un-mysterious. Only the roof is late and Tudor. Pay the Chapel another visit later as you have still only absorbed half of what it has to offer.

The Elder Lady Chapel, Bristol Cathedral

Bristol Cathedral would not come in anyone's top ten for exterior beauty. It would, however, rank in the top three English cathedrals for interior interest because the Augustinian priests who kept extending it were sophisticated city dwellers, devoted to style and experiment. The building needs to be taken gradually, part by separate part. As an introduction, try the Elder Lady Chapel, which branches off the north transept and is a complete church in itself. A helpful notice at its entrance records that it was built soon after 1215. Abbot David had sent a letter around that time to Wells Cathedral asking if he could borrow a mason-designer trained in the lively, idiosyncratic, Early English Gothic of that cathedral which was, by then, almost complete. The notice describes the Elder Lady Chapel as 'a place of sheer exuberance and fun'. See if you agree.

Our Dundry limestone carves well, but it has none of the rich golden bloom of the Doulting limestone that was used at Wells. As a result the Chapel's first impact is gloomy. It is only on an inspection of the carvings lavished over the north wall and the surviving sectors of the south wall that the alien oddity of thirteenth-century religiosity asserts itself. There are monkeys everywhere. I counted eight and probably missed three or four. Not very kind monkeys either, but mocking and gaping-mouthed. Most churches have a Green Man, with leaves coming from his mouth. Bristol has Green Monkeys and the leaves among which they hide have that same elegant, stylized sinuosity that surfaces in prehistoric Celtic bronze work, mid eighteenth-century Rococo and Art Nouveau of the Edwardian period. Originally the south wall must have been the more figurative. Hunt for a knight slaying a dragon, a goat playing the fiddle for a sceptred monkey, and notice the heads that

swallow each section of the string course below the windows, a very Poitevin trick. Gryphons, doves and monkeys, but where are the Saints, where is the Virgin Mary, what were they playing at? Was it just that fascination with monsters that makes for successful films and TV programmes on dinosaurs? Why link the Virgin Mary with a playful Bestiary?

Would limewash on the flat surfaces and a polish for the Purbeck 'marble' shafting be an improvement? Probably not, but while you are thinking, another productive quest would be to track down, in the vestibule to the Chapter House, what are possibly the two earliest structurally pointed Gothic arches in Britain. Then spend ten minutes in the Eastern Lady Chapel brooding over the last frantic attempt of Decorated Gothic to fight off the tedious verticals and geometry of Perpendicular Gothic. Be in at the death throes of a great style, killed off prematurely. Medieval Bristol was no provincial backwater; it was in the mainstream of European style, but unfortunately with a limited span of concentration.

Bristol Central Library, College Green

The Central Library is a most rewarding building to walk around, brooding and debating over its detail, because it sums up all the timidity and the near-miss quality of Bristol's twentieth-century architecture. It is a good building, but if it had been built in Glasgow it would have been so much better. Charles Rennie Mackintosh designed the Glasgow School of Art in 1896 for a site, sloping quite steeply at the back like our Library, and straining historic forms, in his case medieval Scottish tower houses, through the elongations of the current Arts and Crafts. In Bristol, Charles Holden, working with Percy Adams and Lionel Pearson, designed the Library in 1906, with more than an eye on Mackintosh's School of Art. But in Holden's case the historic form was the weaker, more domestic, Cotswold Tudor vernacular. He had little of Mackintosh's linear genius for drawing out long, agonised lines of buttress and latticed oriel window to create sharp, memorable images.

Look at the back of the Library, down the hill. Where Mackintosh created a wonderful cliff of vertical lines, Holden missed his chances with shallow central pilaster strips, windows too small and too few for rhythm and an inappropriate Cotswold cottage flat in the basement for the caretaker. On the narrow east façade to the Norman gatehouse Holden's volumetric stairwell is simple, confident and successful. To the north he fell back onto symmetry and chequer-board patterning, as in Ernest Gimson's inlaid furniture, more Art Deco than sinuous Art Nouveau. Holden's instincts were to move away from decoration towards a functional simplicity. Not surprisingly in the 1930s he would be happy designing those austerely Germanic, much praised London Underground stations at Arnos Grove, Boston Manor and Southgate. In 1906 he was an early Modernist constrained by the neighbouring historic buildings to respect, rather than escape from, an historicist decorative tradition.

The sculpture over the oriels on Holden's north front could have saved the elevation from mediocrity, but Charles Pibworth's figures representing the rise of English literature are conventionally modelled and grouped as on a church porch. Inside, however, Holden went for a modified Byzantine for the Entrance Hall, no mosaics but striped Greek Cippolino marble facing and Irish Green for the capitals. It works impressively and his shallow, broadly circling stairs are a pleasure to climb. But then, inexplicably, for the Reading Room he reverted to a blowsy Beaux Arts classicism, unrelated to anything that had gone before.

In 1964 Albert Clarke added a western extension in a timid paraphrase of Holden. Its top floor was begun but never completed. Very recently has come a trendy coffee room with monstrous silver ventilation pipes, in Richard Rogers' high camp, techno-moderno, set above crimson walls and spindly steel furnishings.

City of Bristol College, College Green Centre, St George's Road

When Ian Nickels, chief architect of the Unite practice, came in 1998 to design the new College Green Centre he found himself dealing with a typically Bristolian set of problems. The site was long, narrow and steeply sloping.

It was overlooked by a large block of Pennant stone flats, St George's House, many of whose occupants were members of the highly active Brandon Hill Residents' Association with strong views about the character of the neighbourhood and its future development. On its south side the site commanded an area of almost totemic nostalgia value to the city: a harbour teeming with historic maritime links. The future building would be squashed between St George's Road and the busy Anchor Road.

Nickels and his project manager, Geoff Haslam, had to work to the usual tight budget for such public works, respect traffic needs and still provide characterful premises for 2,400 students and staff in an area of 11,500 square metres. So, very wisely, the College appointed a consultant, Pete Milner, to coordinate art works, and set aside funds to commission artists who could lavish enough symbolic and whimsical decorative detail on the buildings to make students forget any cost cutting. The building opened to students in October 2000, and was officially opened by Tony Blair on 9 January 2001.

The Centre has an ocean liner as its underlying theme, hence Steve Joyce's twin sextant-styled lamps flanking the entrance and the stern-like bulge of the central bow. A Pennant stone base responds to the flats opposite and the colour panels are slatey blue for marine reference and terracotta for Brandon Hill clay. In the courtyard, glazed staircase towers and a dramatic peaked canopy modify the claustrophobia. That canopy shelters a spiral drum route down to the car-bicycle park and, as a modish extra, it also shelters a pit for those

pariahs of political correctness: student smokers, while to cheer them up the walls of the spiral are covered by Linda Clark's river of ceramic, studded with bottles. Each of these contains a message of hope such as: 'La vie c'est un voyage, pas une destination', all very apposite for dedicated smokers.

On the next level down is the refectory, designed, following a student competition, on a ship's engine room; and at the Anchor Road entrance is Steve Joyce's aluminium floor etched with shipping lanes, plans of ships and sea map motifs based on Battery Point, Portishead. Conor Wilson's undulating brick 'water wave' sculpture is at the base of the stairs and the building's Anchor Road façade is frankly modern with welcoming wide windows. On each floor of the staircase towers there are attractive waiting areas, retro-styled like refugees from TV's *Happy Days*, with circles of seats, snack dispensers and Vicki Davidson's decorative panels. It is not a great building, but a determinedly humane one and it will be interesting to see how it weathers with time.

The Old Police Station, Jacob's Wells Road

The Old Police Station is a reminder of the trauma that hit polite Bristol society after the Reform Bill Riots of 1831. It must have seemed that at long last the French Revolution had spread to England. With the Bishop's Palace in flames, the Mayor escaping from his Lodgings on Queen Square by climbing out onto the gutters to reach the house next door, the Yeomanry uncertain of their duty and the colliers of Kingswood on the rampage, Bristol's establishment took to the hills. They had already built themselves a genteel new suburb up on Clifton Down as far away from the labouring classes as they could get. Then, as their Maginot Line of defence, they constructed four new police stations – this one at Hotwells, the City Guardhouse, and others at Bedminster and St Phillips – and garrisoned them generously. This 1836 police station on the side of Brandon Hill is the only survivor of that panic, raised as a control point to cover the docks and discipline drunken sailors.

Life here in those early days was not far removed from that of soldiers in a barracks; there was a whole armoury of cutlasses in one cupboard for hand-to-hand operations. Up the stairs on the left was the duty sergeant's office where the constables would be told their duty rounds, often involving a twenty-mile tramp in one day. The bigger room upstairs was originally both the dormitory and the drill room for young constables; later it was turned into a skittle alley. Down in the basement the little window allowed the man on duty to keep an eye on the prisoners in the two cells. They were kept there for only one night before being moved on to the Bridewell, but one man still managed to hang himself and is said to haunt occasionally: a brief shadow glimpsed only out of the corner of the eye. The cells were used until a big drugs raid at the Three Tuns pub in the 1960s brought in a number of suspects on such a cold night that they had to spend the dark hours running round the yard to keep warm. After that the cells were deemed unfit for human occupation and they were left to the ghost.

When the police abandoned the station in 1967, Queen Elizabeth's Hospital School took over for a time using it as their art and music department. Before the Avon Wildlife Trust moved into the building in 1986 there was a brief, tawdrily glamorous interval when the Baghwan Rajneesh people set up a bar and decorated the place with a plastic palm tree for local colour.

As you leave spare a thought for Jim, who is buried in the front garden. Jim was an heroic terrier who defended and saved the life of the constable he was accompanying on his night beat. Policeman and dog were both savagely attacked and Jim's leg was broken, but he escaped to bring back help. A climbing rose has been planted over his tomb.

Queen Elizabeth's Hospital, Berkeley Place

At the end of a general inspection carried out in 1961 HM inspectors described the boys of QEH as characterised by 'a pleasantly rugged independence'. It was a shrewd generalisation on a school of distinctive character, and it is tempting to speculate that the 'rugged independence' resulted from their being educated in that forbidding Victorian block, pitched uncompromisingly across the slopes of Brandon Hill. One of the many remarkable things about QEH is that a building designed in 1847 to board and educate some 100 orphans or boys of poor parents is still able, by one device or other of sideways expansion, to function in the twenty-first century as a popular independent school with seventy boarders and almost 400 day boys.

A rich Bristol soap manufacturer, John Carr, left money in his 1586 will to found 'the hospital or place for the bringing up of poor children or orphans...The Mayor and community of Bristol to be patrons and guides'. In 1590 Queen Elizabeth signed for it possibly the most handsomely illustrated Charter of her reign, and for 200 years, based in St Bartholomew's at the foot of Christmas Steps, it turned out clerks to work in city offices. When its land endowments prospered a move was proposed in 1847 to the healthier site it still occupies, and Thomas Foster designed a block in old-fashioned Regency Gothic for a modest £21,000. Behind its grim pseudo-Tudor walls a technically advanced cast-iron supporting structure is concealed, and a seventeenth-century statue of a scholar in full uniform was brought up from St Bartholomew's to be placed in the fine entrance hall as a reminder of the past.

As late as 1920 QEH was still no more than a well disciplined secondary-modern boarding school, passing its best students on to Bristol Grammar when they were fifteen.

Then in 1921 it became a direct grant school, as it should have done decades earlier, and soon began to expand and flourish. In 1939 it was all set for a move out to occupy Vanbrugh's King's Weston House, but the war intervened. Nevertheless, until 1950, the King's Weston project was still alive, and in 1972 another move was proposed out to a site in Brislington. Instead, between 1975 and 1977, an ambitious building programme was undertaken of revising, dividing and extending the old buildings, the boarders moving out into Berkeley Place. Because Red Maids' School has always been its twin-sister establishment it has not gone co-educational. QEH has now settled into a strong conservative affection for its Foster premises, as imaginatively improved and adapted with a splendid modern theatre: a true 'City School' at the heart of Bristol rather than some tame suburban compromise.

Underfall Yard, Cumberland Road

The Underfall Yard is quite unlike any other site on the Open Doors list. In a ship repair yard tucked away behind the Nova Scotia pub on Cumberland Basin an enormous piece of Victorian engineering cleverness is still thumping and pumping away, doing dramatic things every few minutes to delight the onlooker. Down a narrow cart entry off Avon Crescent there is a gaunt tower of harsh red brick. This is the Hydraulic Engine House of 1888 and the tower originally contained the accumulator which now works in the open on the side of it, rising and falling at intervals to set hidden pumps to work in the long range behind the tower. The pounding of the hidden machinery and the apparently erratic rising and juddering of the great steel canister are an experience in themselves, quite apart from the enchanting, small-scale maritime activity of dry docks and repair sheds that is going on all around the monstrous toy. When I made my visit I was lucky enough to catch the *Matthew*, the John Cabot replica, in dry dock on the Patent Slip for a check-up, but there is always activity to evoke what Bristol was once about in its glory days.

That Underfall Pump demands an explanation. Why this repetitive activity on such an apparently tranquil inland water? Briefly, the Underfall was one of several cures for the inadequacy of the Overfall. Between 1804 and 1809 the engineer, William Jessop, had diverted the Avon into the New Cut and created, in its old course, the Floating Harbour by putting a big dam across it at the west end of the Cumberland Basin. A weir back at Netham Road diverted some water along The Feeder into this harbour and that was allowed to escape across the Overfall, an ordinary over-the-top sluice. But this was not enough of an escape route to clear the Floating Harbour of sewage, so the centre of Bristol began to smell very badly indeed. Isambard Kingdom

Brunel was consulted in 1834 and 1842 and he devised a drag boat to scrape the filth to the centre of the harbour. Later, in 1887, when a number of swing bridges had been built across the harbour, a hydraulic power system was required to work these and to open and close the lock gates which, until then, had been hand operated. To provide that power the Hydraulic Engine House was built in the Underfall Yard. Now, when the bridges are only swung infrequently, this compressed air pump still functions to force filth and surplus water out under the sluice. It works well, powered originally by steam and now by electricity. That big canister produces the pressure in its downward drop. The actual sluice is an inconspicuous brick structure a little further on by the water's edge, at a point that offers wonderful views across the basin to the recent dockside development of Poole's Wharf and the coloured terraces of Victorian Cliftonwood on the hill slope above.

On Open Doors days some of the workshops still in use will be open with much of the original Victorian machinery, particularly the Blacksmith's Shop and the Pump House.

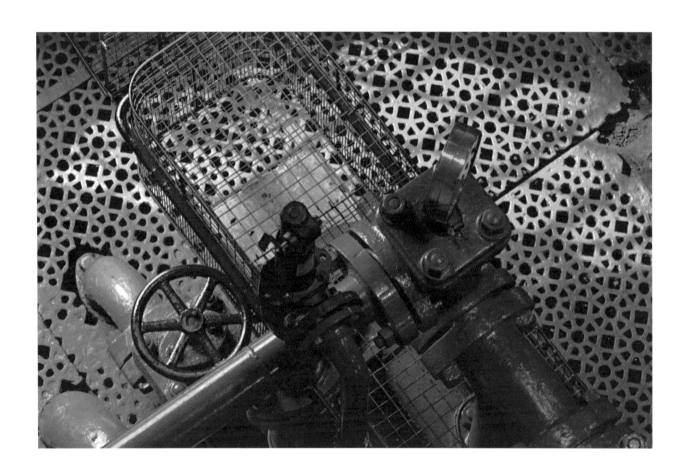

Lloyds TSB, Canon's Marsh

It is easy to be wise after an event. When this sprawling complex of crescent and circle was first proposed in the 1980s it seemed just the project to power the regeneration of that miserable dockside area. Lloyds was a big name, Post-modern architecture was the style of the decade, and Ove Arup was a prestigious firm, one likely to balance a witty play on historic motifs, classical for preference, with slick modern design. The initial drawings promised a confident gesture on a run-down site, a memorable building with Palladian or even Baroque references, exactly the safe compromise that Bristol tends to favour. But what we should have seen was that harboursides are essentially functional areas that do not suit the monumental. Dockside buildings, more than any others, need to be workmanlike, even gritty, and to relate functionally to the water. They do not usually accord happily with a grand piazza like that in front of St Peter's in Rome.

Wit was the essence of Post-modern styling and that is another problem with Lloyds. A joke repeated thirty or more times on the crescent and the circle soon stops being funny. Arup's joke was to have classical columns, but then not give them capitals. Instead of supporting an entablature or cornice they fade out into brown metal cylinders in an attic vacancy, with a little fuzz of spikes to prevent pigeons perching. A weak Meccano diagonal of struts with no obvious function is used ornamentally to fill the gap between the first and second floors. Then, as if aware that tedium was setting in, the architects pitched four different colours and textures of stone or concrete into the sandwich of three storeys.

That piazza and the surrounding wilderness of car-parks builds up the expectation that this is a major piece of architecture making an important statement, but the complex has neither a vertical element to pull its profile together, nor any fine detail to satisfy closer inspection.

A committed Post-modernist like Robert Venturi, working on his Sainsbury Wing to the National Gallery, knew that a classical column would not make a convincing reference without the almost subliminal fine lines of the 'correct' classical orders: abacus, astragal, fillet and the rest. Arup thought that rough, plain cylinders could pass for witty columns, but here they just look cheap and under-educated. Inside the mood switches to minimalist Scandinavian with subtle cream walls and light woods.

There could be a solution. Sweep away the skate-boarders' piazza and cram it with two harbour lanes of higgledy-piggledy houses and small flats; make it an expensive mews development with moorings to the rear. Lloyds could rise up over the top of them like the Pantheon over the ordinary streets of Rome. It would make money and humanize a half-dead area; but would our permanently hung Council ever have the nerve to push through such a bold scheme?

Redcliffe Caves, Phoenix Wharf

The truth about Bristol's mysterious Redcliffe Caves is that there is nothing mysterious about them. For hundreds of years Bristol made money by making and selling glass. There were as many as ten big funnel-shaped glass furnaces in the stretch from Brandon Hill to St Philip's Marsh, polluting the valley air with sooty black smoke. To see how big they were take a look at the brick base of one up Prewett Street, where it has been turned into an hotel's restaurant.

Most of this glass, Bristol Blue excepted, and that was originally made out near Pensford, was rough stuff for beer bottles and the like. But it all needed fine sand in the manufacture and the hill under Redcliffe Parade, first named Addercliff Down, had a belt of that sand. As far back as the thirteenth century, for Bristol has always been an industrial city, the glass-makers mined their way in under the Addercliff, starting from the wharf where the new *Matthew* was built, leaving pillars of the sandstone to support the houses built on Guinea Lane and, of course, St Mary Redcliffe Church itself. Some accounts have it that at certain areas in the caves you can hear St Mary's organ playing.

Certainly the maze of tunnels, which is what they really are, not caves, is extensive and not perfectly charted. This is because some property owners on the hill above laid legitimate legal claim to the tunnels immediately underneath them and walled some galleries up for privacy. Once in World War II a German bomb hit a house on Redcliffe Parade and went right through its coal cellar into the tunnels beneath. Apparently the old miners sometimes left only a three-foot thickness in the roof over their tunnels. One octagonal chamber has eight pillars around its sides and the ninth in its centre contains the shaft of a well dug down from the house above.

It is claimed that when the New Cut river was dug in 1804 one of the caves was sliced through and each end had to be walled up. There was another cave exit in the 1665 Quakers' Burial Ground off the Redcliffe traffic roundabout. That was where a hermit called John Sparkes was housed by Thomas, Lord Berkeley in 1346 to pray for his soul. There was possibly a tunnel connection with St John's Priory above it. One catacomb branched off from Alfred's or King's Quay and a second from behind Redcliffe Wharf. Bristol City Council bought the first in 1912 and the second in 1950. Then, in the late 1980s, there was a scheme to turn the Caves into an attraction incorporating a new hotel and restaurant – 200,000 visitors a year were projected – but it never came to anything. When I last went in I bumped my head in one tunnel quite badly, so never go in hoping to rely on someone else's torch.

The Georgian House, Great George Street

The Georgian House is one of an elegantly dull foursome, numbers 3, 23 and 25 are the others, that were built around 1788 by William Paty in the improved, basically neo-Classical, austerity which was spreading out from London. William, son of the now elderly Thomas, had just returned from an apprenticeship in the capital. Only the servants' basement floor is of rough Pennant stone; the ground floor is of rusticated Bath stone, then there is sleek Bath stone ashlar all the way up, the windows simply sliced into the wall with no architraves or framing. This reserved, bourgeois house, based upon a sugar manufactory fortune, was where Wordsworth first became friendly with Coleridge. So in that sense the house, or the Pinney family who owned it, fired off the Romantic movement with all the revolutionary changes that it involved in social thinking and attitudes to Nature.

That first room on the left should not have been opened up to the hall in the twentieth century simply to make a visual impact, but it does have three fine bookcases with broken pediments that are original to the premises. Almost all the other excellent furnishings have been brought in and are perhaps just a shade too fine. On the other hand someone who could afford 13 guineas to line that chimney-piece with 'Blue John', a scarce Derbyshire amethystine quartz, was not short of money.

Hidden away on the extreme right of this and on every floor above it are the cramped, dark servants' stairs intended to keep the staff of probably four out of sight of the gentry as they serviced the house, cleaning and carrying. Oddly these stairs do not go right down to the kitchen. This is because John Pinney was addicted to a cold plunge every morning, and where the stairs should have connected with the kitchens is his deep, gloomy plunge bath, a most atmospheric item. The servants must have had to avert their eyes from the master in the nude each breakfast time.

Up on the first floor, in the front room on the left, is an astonishing secretaire bookcase with strange curvaceous tracery. When new it cost a mere £15. It would be hard to price it today for under a quarter of a million. In the big, back drawing room are several paintings that convey how the Avon Gorge must have looked at high tide before the Portway was constructed: more Norwegian fiord than Somerset. One more floor up are the bedrooms where the quality of the cast-iron fire grates, with their light airy cupid figures, is most impressive. In contrast, the glass in the twelve-pane sashes is extremely poor. It is original and dates back to the period before the plate glass process was invented. On the way back down the stone staircase it is worth reflecting upon what a restrictive and confining machine for living in this house must have been, every room with a precise function; and yet this severe classical box was the social birthplace of Romantic poetry.

25

The Red Lodge, Park Row

People who believe that simplicity is the essence of good art and fine building should give the Red Lodge a wide berth. It is, however, a wonderful place, indeed one of the best interiors in England to see whether you can cope with Elizabethan and Jacobean art, a truly native phenomenon, at its wildest and richest. Dating of the Red Lodge and its interior decoration is another minefield. Most authorities, lured by the sophistication of the woodwork, place it as at least post-1580. But Sir John Young began the Great House, in whose gardens the Red Lodge and its lost twin would stand, back in 1568 in preparation for Queen Elizabeth's visit to Bristol in 1574. She did stay in the Great House (on the site of the Colston Hall) and the visit was a whirl of lavish entertainments. Twin garden lodges were virtually essential to superior social activities from the time of Henry VIII onwards, so surely Sir John would have had his twin lodges ready by 1574. That is not the end of the problems. The superb ceiling and panelling of the Great Oak Room on the first floor, easily the richest in Bristol if not in the country, is often dated to between 1585 and 1600; but its strapwork ceiling is very similar to that which was in Langton Mansion on Welsh Back and that was clearly dated 1628.

There is another indication of Jacobean rather than Elizabethan date. The inner, or draught-excluding, porch in the Great Oak Room is so exotic in its wood carving that it makes the rest of that glorious room look positively modest, and the carving on the porch does seem to include a number of American Red Indians. But the successful colonization of Virginia, which would have made Red Indian head-dresses familiar to Bristol carvers, took place in James I's reign, not Elizabeth's. A further confusion to the unwary is that the panelling in the room on the ground floor has been brought in from St Michael's Rectory.

The wisest course is to ignore this scholarly subtlety and just revel in the delicate stonework, riotous wood carving and the paintings which are interesting as records of their time rather than beautiful. From a patriotic point of view it is regrettable that English painters of the period were so inferior in the handling of perspective or facial likenesses to their Dutch and Italian contemporaries. Italy's Renaissance was at its peak by 1450; ours had hardly got going 200 years later. Give the chimney-piece in the Great Oak Room your extra attention. It is my personal theory that the English gentry, robbed by the Protestant Reformation of the chance to spend money on great altarpieces, turned to chimney-pieces as a domestic substitute with heraldry and figures of the noble virtues standing in for the Crucifixion and the Catholic saints. Apply that theory to the alabaster carving of the Great Oak Room chimney-piece over-mantel and it seems to make sense. At least two distinct carvers, both masters, have been working together. Before you leave spend a moment in the recreated Tudor knot garden with its authentic planting of herbs.

26

The Savages' Wigwam, Red Lodge, Lodge Street

The Bristol Savages are 'provincial' in the very best sense of that word, a remarkable survival of rowdy, convivial Edwardian aestheticism – art with handlebar moustaches and comic recitations. Strictly speaking they began in Victoria's reign, in 1894 when Ernest Ehlers and four other artists, his 'brothers of the brush', began meeting once a week in a ramshackle conservatory on Portland Street to knock back a bottle of whisky, sketch for two hours on a given theme, like 'Solitude', 'Market Day', 'The Vision Splendid' or 'Haunted', all very *Yellow Book* in feeling, then criticise each other's work. As an evening out for the heartier brand of aesthete these meetings proved popular. The venues grew more ambitious and in 1904 'The Savages' was adopted as the club's title after the Chairman had observed one evening that they all behaved like them. Their first annual exhibition of work was held in 1905 at an auctioneers in Broad Street, and in 1907 their first 'Wigwam' was set up in a big room at Brandon Cottage and decorated in a style appropriate to a tribe of Red Indians.

That was where the tradition grew up of having an hour or two of entertainment for members and guests after the sketching session: an elaboration of the original 'knees-up' with songs, poems and comic renditions. Minutes were read before each session with ribald interjections as part of the fun. When, in 1919, the Red Lodge came on the market, the Savages' second founder, Brother Savage Fuller Eberle, known as 'Bongie', persuaded a group of wealthy members to buy it and restore it to its former Elizabethan glory. As a headquarters for the Tribe, a new Wigwam was built in the back garden of the Red Lodge, designed like a tithe barn by the Bristol artist-historian-architect, C F W Dening, himself a Brother Savage. As an inauguration ceremony the Savages' annual dinner was held in the new Wigwam on 24 April 1920, with 180 members and guests gorging themselves.

Sketching sessions continued to be taken very seriously before each Wednesday meeting and membership was raised from 200 to 300 to cover expenses. Needless to say not all those 300 were active artists, but in a city like Bristol there was always a healthy waiting list of men anxious to join in the fun. Artist members wear red lapel feathers, entertainers wear blue, and lay members wear green feathers. Ladies' nights and an annual service in the Lord Mayor's Chapel became further traditional fixtures. The exotic collection of weapons, paintings, curios and sketches around the walls have all been contributed by Brother Savages over the years. Few art auctions in the city go by without some paintings by Savages, pleasant seascapes or views of pastoral landscapes, appearing in the sales catalogues. They are the 'amateur' artists who keep the title of 'artist' plausible and honourable in these days when 'professional' artists have turned to abstracts and sensational gimmickry.

27

The Wills Memorial Tower, Queen's Road

Behind that quite modest tower entrance at the top of Park Street is an astonishing truncated cathedral, improbably high, crammed with an inappropriate avalanche of steps, yet blessed with perfect acoustics for carol singing. Visually and stylistically the Wills Memorial Tower makes no kind of sense. This last confident flowering of the secular Gothic Revival was contemporary with the rising Art Deco skyscrapers of New York. To understand its aggressive triumphalism start at the bottom of Park Street where Unity Street branches off. There, on the right-hand side, is a dilapidated brick building. That was the rival establishment, the Tory and Anglican Merchant Venturers' Technical College which the Liberal and Non-Conformist 'University College' up the hill defeated in an academic race to win, in 1909, a Royal Charter making it autonomous.

It had been a close-run finish but, when the tobacco multi-millionaire, Henry Overton Wills, promised the University College an endowment of £100,000 in 1908, that decided the Liberal Government. Then, however, in a foolish show of patronage and arrogance, the new University celebrated by awarding seventy honorary degrees at one convocation and sacking three professors from their chairs. Recriminations and bad feelings resulted, honours had been cheapened and standards threatened. So, when the first Chancellor, Henry Wills, died his sons Henry and George decided on a positive relaunch for the University by funding a great Memorial Tower on the site of the old Blind Asylum and Rifle Drill Hall.

The Vice-Chancellor had hoped for a modern ferro-concrete structure, but the Wills brothers' preferred architect, George (later Sir George) Oatley, told his patrons that, if they wanted their tower to last 400 years, it would have to be built of stone and, to realise Oatley's Puginesque

vision of a crown of towers on the hilltop, should be Gothic in style. Designed in 1911-14, but delayed by the Great War, the tower went up between 1919 and 1925, costing over £500,000. It is resounding in its impact, but too broad for its height. That stumpiness is explained by the breadth and scale of the entrance hall with its Perpendicular Gothic windows fifty feet high and the seventy-two feet high fan vaulting. In effect, four bays have been cut off from the eighty-foot high King's College Chapel, Cambridge to function merely as a stunning grand staircase. The Non-Conformists had stolen the Anglicans' clothes.

Oatley did not skimp on the depth of the mouldings in those crisp panelled walls and his vault is structural, but there is none of the inventive Arts and Crafts detail that enriches the tower of his 1929 Physics Laboratory. Enjoy the superbly lettered plaque commemorating the opening by King George. It describes the monarch as 'George Vth', which was considered a terrible solecism at the time; but the final score in Bristol's centuries-old political football match was Liberals 1, Tories 0.

28

Eastern Orthodox Church, University Road

By a complete twist of religious affiliations and geography it is quite appropriate that an Orthodox congregation should be occupying a Gothic building in University Road, even though Orthodoxy is usually associated with the round arches and domes of Byzantine architecture. The Church of the Nativity of the Mother of God is home, not to a Greek or even a Russian congregation, but to the Autocephalous Polish Orthodox Church, and Poland's architectural history, like that of western Europe, has been pre-eminently Gothic as any visitor to Crakow will confirm. The church was originally built in 1888 for George Irvine's charismatic Presbyterians, a sect which had adopted Roman Catholic rites in expectation of the Second Coming. Their cathedral and administrative centre was the noble Gothic church in Gordon Square, Bloomsbury. That has now become London University's Chaplaincy Centre. The first Irvingite church in Bristol was St Mary-on-the-Quay. As the community in their second church in University Road dwindled it was taken over by Bristol's Polish and Ukrainian Orthodox communities.

A sizeable part of Poland was absorbed into the Russian empire after the various eighteenth-century partitions of that unlucky country, and large numbers of Poles in that Russian sector became converted from Catholicism to Orthodoxy. After Germany and Russia invaded Poland in 1939 many Orthodox Poles took refuge in this country.

A Bristol parish of Orthodox believers held its first celebration of their liturgy in the Chapter House of Bristol Cathedral on 12 September 1948 when Archbishop Sawa of Grodno agreed to send a priest to Bristol every month to celebrate vespers on a Saturday evening and the liturgy on Sunday morning. Initially four national groups – Poles, Russians, Ukranians and Serbs – took part in these services in the Church Hall of St John, Bedminster. It was Father Nicholas Behr who found the present building and converted it from Irvingite to Orthodox usage. The liturgy was first celebrated here on Palm Sunday 1968, an event recorded on BBC TV.

Over the next few years more and more English joined the congregation and by 1979 the choir was singing beautifully in both English and Polish. Father Nicholas supported himself as a worker priest by carpentry for the twenty-two years of his ministry. In the 1990s more Russian émigrés began to join the parish, and the last of the original Polish founder members died in 1996. In 1997 the Archdiocese of Thyateira assumed sole priestly and pastoral care, in the same year the Ukranian Orthodox began co-celebrating and Slavonic vespers were also held. Relations with the Anglican Fellowship of SS Alban and Sergius have always been warm. September 1994 saw between 800 and 1,000 Open Doors visitors coming in to enjoy the surprising novelty of icons and an iconostasis in a Victorian Gothic Revival building.

29

Bristol Grammar School, Woodland Road

The Great Hall that John Foster and Joseph Wood designed to re-house Bristol's Grammar School has been described, fairly enough, as 'Gothic of the debased or Tudor style'. It is very Bristolian in its reliance on the polychromatic play of creamy Bath limestone dressings up and down the walls of red Brandon Hill sandstone. There was hope, when the building began in 1875, that stone from the site would have enough iron in it to justify smelting. If it had then the Great Hall would not have stood on the edge of a disastrously sloping playing field, but a quarry. The School's charismatic, dictatorial headmaster at that time, John William Caldicott, would not have minded much, as he was far more interested in Oxford and Cambridge scholarships than football or rugby.

Foster and Wood conceived the new building in its extraordinarily impractical form of one huge 50-foot high, 140-foot long, 50-foot broad hall with an open pitch-pine crown post roof on top of a mere eight classrooms to humour Caldicott. He had been taught at King Edward's School, Birmingham, which had been built to the same old-fashioned plan. With as many as eighteen classes all going on in one big room he could keep an eye on the teachers and the boys. He claimed that a small classroom 'impairs the spirit of unity in the School' and wasted time as the boys moved from one room to another or were left alone for a minute or two. Caldicott was a strict disciplinarian and a 'crammer'.

It would take another forty years for the Grammar School to recover from his pig-headedness, but he had fought hard to get the money for the rebuilding from the Charity Trustees so he was able to have his own way, going down as the School's 'second founder', after the first founder, Robert Thorne, in Henry VIII's reign. As so often in Bristol the Wills family were major benefactors. They paid for the oriel window and presented the clock on that lean tower which gives a very necessary vertical note to the long horizontals of the windows. Lord Winterstoke also gave the organ. Canopies were added later to the masters' stalls in an attempt to focus the boys' attention in the confusion of conflicting lessons in Latin, English and Mathematics, all going on at the same time and in the same room. To be fair the Great Hall with its soaring roof is ideal for those morning assemblies that have given most pupils a strong sense of corporate loyalty, and subsequent headmasters have improvised ingeniously on the cramped Victorian site. Homework no longer takes six hours every evening as it did in Caldicott's day and the new sports and health centre is state-of-the-art.

30

The Royal Fort, Tyndall's Park

Perhaps it is wrong in this account of near fifty Open Doors buildings to have a favourite, but it would be hard to find interiors behind any of the other 'open doors' to rival the suite of entertainment rooms that Thomas Paty and his team of wood carvers, plasterers and masons created for the wealthy Thomas Tyndall and his young wife, Alicia, between 1758 and 1762 at the Royal Fort. These, together with the choir of the Cathedral and the north porch of St Mary Redcliffe, are Bristol's three architectural stars.

Because the American-born James Bridges made the wooden model for the Royal Fort, still preserved in the house, authorities persist in describing him as the architect despite the fact that all three façades of the house are in entirely different styles and that a contemporary poem explicitly names three architects: Thomas Paty, John Wallis and Bridges as equally responsible. Myths die hard, but walk around the Fort, starting with the entrance front and, in sequence, the three styles are late Baroque, Palladian and canted-bay Rococo. Bridges simply tied unifying plat bands and sill bands around them.

Inside, after the masculine entrance hall in relatively sober, though still fine, Palladian plasterwork with a warlike Doric frieze, the other three principal rooms are exquisitely feminine and Rococo. The first door on the right leads to the Drawing Room, Arcadian in its decorative theme of shepherd and shepherdess, but with long-necked ho-ho birds, a Chinese motif, flying across the corners of the ceiling amidst twining branches in Rococo S-curves. The family portrait on the wall is of Thomas Tyndall with his second wife and their children. A little Boudoir opens off from this room. Next comes the Eating Room. Here the theme is one of shooting and wildlife. An eagle threatens a bird on the ceiling, squirrels run along branches and Paty's own skill as a wood carver is demonstrated in the trophy of guns and nets above the chimney-piece and in the enchanting fantasy of scrolls and festoons and painting of the door-case: a French design, but culled from Thomas Johnson's 1758 *One Hundred and Fifty New Designs*. Paty was paid £17.10s for the trophies and £24 for the door-case.

Most celebrated is the Staircase Hall. The cantilever staircase has an ironwork balustrade which mirrors the serpentine curves of the plasterwork. Here the plasterers have been inspired by the designs of Chinese wallpaper to create vines which hold, not simply bunches of grapes, but further fantasy worlds of Willow Pattern land. There are shepherds with goats, foxes slyly pursuing birds, ruined towers and floating islands. It would be satisfying to credit the Irish plasterer, Thomas Stocking, with the work but, although he is associated with the Paty team elsewhere in the city, his name is not mentioned in the Royal Fort accounts. The rooms upstairs are plain in comparison with these imaginative interiors. Alicia Tyndall died tragically young in 1764 and she appears to have been the inspiration behind this, the liveliest Rococo plasterwork in England.

31

The Royal West of England Academy, Queen's Road

While crying over spilt milk is unprofitable it is still reasonable to express regret that Charles Underwood's 1852 Greek Ionic design for the proposed new Academy was rejected in favour of John Henry Hirst's Germano-Italianate scheme, based on the Palazzo Barberini in Rome and the Alte Pinakothek at Munich. Underwood's six Ionic columns would have responded splendidly to the eight Corinthian columns of Charles Dyer's Victoria Rooms across the road, giving a real coherence to this gateway to classical Clifton. But Hirst had been touring the new academy buildings of Germany and Austria and he had overwhelmed his fellow members of the Bristol Society of Architects in a lecture which he gave in November 1852. The Germans had gone Italianate and Bristol should follow.

In the uneasy compromise that followed Hirst designed the façade and Underwood designed the rooms behind it with the School of Art on the ground floor and the quite separate galleries of the artists' Academy on the floor above, reached by a double flight of steps. By 1905 these arrangements had come to be considered divisive and insufficiently grand. The elaborate, even palatial, reconstruction scheme which went forward between 1908 and 1913, with a two-storey, domed entrance hall approached from ground level, was the confused but undeniably sumptuous result. Henry Dare Bryan, aided by George Oatley, drew up the first scheme, Silcock and Reay revised it when they took over as architects after Dare Bryan's death in 1909. Their relatively minor alterations resulted in sub-Grecian notes of key frets and anthemions in the place of Dare Bryan's Beaux Arts classicism, but what survived and can be enjoyed today is the play of marble panelling: the light green fields of Amialto veined with black and the sombre 'antique black' of the staircase.

This subdued richness, more gentlemen's club than art gallery, rises into the cheerful brilliance of Walter Crane's murals – *Painting*, *Sculpture*, *Craftsmanship* and *Architecture* – in the lunettes of the dome. Silcock & Reay had wanted the murals to be painted by a protégé, a Mr Preston, but three adjudicating professors of the Royal College of Art in South Kensington opted for Crane, as the more famous and accomplished. Crane's first two panels, oil on canvas, Painting and Craftsmanship, are radiant in colour, sensuous and appealing for all their stiffly posed didactic symbolism; naked Truth, a girl, is painted by a muscular young artist, peacocks, orange trees and temples make up an evocative backdrop. Only these two were in place when George V opened the new entrance hall in 1913. Then the dying artist fell into a more sombre mood, muddy purples infuse the palettes of Craftsmanship and Architecture, though the latter has the liveliest composition of the four. In 1916 Walter Crane died and these are his impressive swan song.

32

Bristol & West, Temple Back East

Over the last five years a new quarter of Bristol has sprung up in the wasteland between Temple Meads Station and the Floating Harbour. It may be a testimonial to the aesthetic ineptitude of the planners and the macho competitive instincts of the architects, but it cannot be ignored. Bristol & West have, very bravely, thrown their HQ into the Open Doors options. Instead of hurrying past along Temple Way with your eyes averted, take the plunge, go down Avon Street to where the former BDC Marketing Centre – that miracle of small modernist styling by the Alec French Partnership – stands empty and unused by the ugly bank of the Floating Harbour. This nautical-style, re-usable building cries out to be turned into a dashing restaurant and café on a tree-lined quay.

Nevertheless, next to the Marketing Centre the Wibbly (as opposed to the Wobbly) bridge leaps out on its exhilarating S-bend curve across the brown water and lands office workers by the Ferry Stop for Temple Meads Station. Now the incredible mix of unneighbourly styles and building materials that make up Temple Square is spread out for your inspection. To be fair it is a great deal livelier and more interesting than the tedious façades that went up around Broadmead after the war. Given a few additions on a different scale to humanize the area, a row of two-storey houses and a scatter of small shopping arcades, it might work, if not well, then at least acceptably.

Everything on your right is the Bristol & West HQ, designed by Chapman Taylor & Stride Treglown between 1997 and 2000. This is one of its four separate elevations; again to give the building its due, it has no squalid rear premises like those in Broadmead. Instead a vast butterfly plan façade with a Flash Gordon glazed centre-piece expands its wings above the water. On the apex of the roof is a metal sculpture of a Pelorus, an instrument for measuring distances at sea, which was named after Hannibal's pilot. When architects despair of expressive decorative detail for their elevations they tend to go for a sandwich of contrasting materials. It is the Post-modernist way out of a design problem, and so Bristol & West rises from Pennant stone with Bath stone dressings to a gaudy yellow brick level and ends in a wall of harsh red brick. Better, again, than slabs of grey concrete. On the entrance front, once you have passed the skeletal ironwork bull and beetle sculpture in the Square, the reception area lies behind a towering wall of glass and steel. In the atrium two lifts whiz up and down on visible metal ropes and all around, as in some Californian hotel of the 1930s, are billowing white balconies in curvaceous swirls of oddly soft profile. The black leather chairs have wonderfully springy backs and the high-tech turnstiles make a futuristic geometric statement. All of this has a brash charm, but the absence of any regional or national stylistic reference means that we could be anywhere in the world.

33

Temple Meads Station

It is only now, in the twenty-first century, that Bristol is beginning to cope with Isambard Kingdom Brunel's disastrous siting of the terminus for his Great Western line from London out in the sticks, almost a mile from the city's commercial centre and two miles from its social centre up on Clifton downs. He had been prevented from building it next to his new Royal Western Hotel, now Brunel House, just behind the present Council House. But at last, with the construction of those self-confident monoliths off Temple Way and around the new Temple Square, Temple Meads Station is becoming socially integrated. Thousands of office workers are actually going to find it convenient.

Brunel does, however, deserve some gratitude for designing, and opening in 1841, a terminus so handsome, with its Perpendicular Gothic entrance building, that no one has ever had the heart to pull it down long after it had ceased to serve much purpose. It is, therefore, the oldest railway terminal in the world and one to be very proud of with its octagonal Tudor turrets, boardroom and flat for the station master. Behind it, even more surprisingly, Brunel's Train Shed with cast-iron columns and wooden box-frame roof, has also survived. The modern Platform 1, where trains from Severn Beach come in, could still be said to utilise it, otherwise it serves ignominiously as a car-park.

In the year when Brunel's terminus was built the terminus of the Bristol and Exeter line opened, in the fiercely competitive spirit of the day, on the other side of the present approach road. A little later, in 1852, S C Fripp built the office block in a blowsy Anglo-Flemish style which still stands, looking rather lost and without purpose. Originally it also had a Brunel wooden shed, but that was pulled down in 1878 when the two stations were amalgamated and the awkwardly curved main station by Matthew Digby Wyatt was constructed to join them and, at the same time, make then both redundant.

Wyatt's station buildings are difficult to love. On the outside they are in a nondescript picturesque manner, vaguely Tudor and built of Pennant stone. Inside, the curve of the tracks makes the perspectives of Francis Cox's diagonally braced iron trusses less satisfying than their scale should have deserved. The brickwork is drab and Railtrack, again a most unloved company, has left as its memorial a curious area of yellow plastic 'marble' tiles on Platform 3 which show up, by their polished cleanliness, the general grime of the floors around them.

A refreshment room, which changes its name and décor every few years, does have a handsome carved Tudor oriel to Digby Wyatt's credit and there is an attractive vista of cast-iron Tudor arches linking the Wyatt and Brunel stations. A few platforms were added by P E Culverhouse in a modest GWR Art Deco in the 1930s. These, platforms 13-15, have recently been restored to use and their waiting room has a mild period charm.

34

St Vincent's Works, Silverthorne Lane

The St Vincent's Works gains enormously by it dismal setting and it was no accident that in the 2001 Open Doors Day this was one of the most visited properties, over a thousand eager Bristolians making the journey to Lysaght's fantasy. First comes a very long dark tunnel under the railway leading into Gas Lane, a narrow gutter between high walls of leprous grey stone. Normal Bristol has been left behind; in its place is a Gothic industrial wasteland, a Mordor of poisoned earth and abandoned factories. But then, suddenly, at the corner with Silverthorne Lane, that improbable vision of Victorian self-confidence and stylistic schitzophrenia comes into view. There are neo-Norman towers and battlements over long ranges of Florentine Renaissance bifora windows, a wild brew of late nineteenth-century Romanesque looking like a palace-fortress in the Ruritanian Alps.

Immediately inside what should be a back entrance is the prodigious dome of golden tiles, an interior richer than the famous William Morris Room in the Victoria and Albert Museum. On the mosaic floor tridents and anchors alternate between dolphins and Bristol's elaborate coat of arms makes the centre-piece. Every visible wall is radiant with tiles, the soffits of the gallery are encrusted with Raphaelesque grotesque work after the style of Walter Crane, and the coffering of the dome itself is painted with a procession of ships from Egyptian galleys, Nelson's *Victory* (with cut-back masts) to the latest steam ironclad battle cruiser (pre-Dreadnought). Tiled stairs sweep up to the gallery with ferocious carved gryphons snarling on the handrail, the central heating radiators are composed of classical Doric pillar-pipes and sinuous copper finger-plates guard every door lock around the octagon, to wages, timekeepers, muniments, stationers and roofing departments.

This was the administration block to John Lysaght Limited. John, a Bristol-educated Irishman, was given a galvanising plant with just seven workers in 1857. He expanded this along Silverthorne Lane to supply half the corrugated iron roofs in Australia with a side-line in buckets. His brother, Thomas Royce Lysaght, was the architect of all this uninhibited display; his plans are in the Bristol Record Office, yet the under-used front door has 'R Milverton Drake, Architect, 1893' carved over it, so the two men must have worked in partnership. If Lysaght favoured Norman Romanesque and Drake preferred the Florentine that could explain the stylistically bizarre design. Even the dates are confused: the plans suggest 1886 while the eclectic styling looks nearer to 1850. It would, however, be very Bristol if this whole glorious complex were hopelessly old-fashioned for its time. The building is now the home of Garrad Hassan and Partners Limited, a firm which gives advice on wind energy, and continues the tradition on the site for advanced engineering.

35

Bristol Blue Glass Workshop, Three Queens' Lane

Most visitors to Venice take the boat trip out to the island of Murano to watch the fascinating dexterity of its Venetian glass blowers. Fewer visitors to Bristol cross Bristol Bridge to hunt down No.5 Three Queens' Lane where the Blue Glass blowers demonstrate similar extraordinary skills in the city's most enjoyable free show: The Theatre of Glass.

Do not expect architectural excitements from Three Queens' Lane. It is not a narrow medieval alley where half-timbered houses lean across to touch each other's window sills. That may once have been its original condition, but now it is a wide road carrying very little traffic and lined by dull industrial premises, one of which, open all down its road front, is the Blue Glass Workshop. The showroom is a dazzle, piled high with delicate antique shapes in three gloriously aggressive transparencies: the celebrated cobalt blue, a delicately washed-out aquamarine, supposedly based upon minerals in Bath's spa water, and 'Cranberry', a Victorian tint aimed at reflecting the flowers of Exmoor. The last two may be a little bogus but are still most seductive.

What is so visually stimulating here is to look across from these covetable sophistications in their glass cases to the rough industrial reality under the same roof, to the rows of roaring 'glory hole' furnaces, the parked motorbikes and the rugged young men casually and confidently crafting refined shapes out of glowing molten gobbets. The nearer you get to the process (and the men seem quite unfazed by audience attention) the more impressive their skills become. Blowing down tubes features less than rolling and whirling the molten glass in the air on long punti irons. It seems impossible that such extrovert violence should result in attenuated glass stems, frilled lips and fragile fluted bowls of eggshell thinness. But then a big black crate takes the eye. It overflows with apparently beautiful glassware, all those highly priced items on display back in the showroom, but these have been thrown down in a heap and rejected. They are the victims of the glass blower's art, apparently perfect, but each one slightly flawed and cast out to be melted down again, aesthetic refugees.

Other large butts hold the raw material, a heap of frit (multicoloured splinters), a mountain of pure glass, like drops of melted ice, waiting for the furnace and the addition of the cobalt oxide that will give it that intense, unmistakable colouring. In the seventeenth century William Cookworthy, a Bristol merchant, acquired the exclusive rights to import a superior cobalt oxide from the Royal Saxon Smalt Works near Dresden, and 300 years ago the 'Nonsuch' glassworks in this same Redcliffe district was producing the Blue Glass fantasies that are still whirling and twisting their way out from Three Queens' Lane today.

36

The Pierian Centre, 27 Portland Square

Among all Open Doors premises No. 27 Portland Square is the one for real architectural enthusiasts. This house is a time capsule of details in wood, stone and plaster preserving exactly the 'before' and 'after' state of the great bank crash of 1793 after war broke out with France, ending Bristol's building boom, and leaving her developers bankrupt with more than a hundred terrace houses here, and in Clifton, empty and unfinished.

Daniel Hague had planned the Square and begun its church, St Paul's, in 1789, the worst possible time, just as the French Revolution was beginning. But he laid out designs for the proposed terraces, allotting ten house sites to the builder, Thomas Pope, later to become City Surveyor, and sixteen to the timber merchant and furniture dealer, James Lockier. A legal release of 26 March 1792 between Lockier and Pope lists the team responsible for constructing the house for the attorney, William Daniel: Richard Webb, Carpenter, Nicholas Cory, House Carpenter, John Clement, Plumber, John Harris, Mason. The Square was named after the 3rd Duke of Portland, who was High Steward of Bristol at the time, and was a most fashionable address for middle-class businessmen.

When the team began work in 1792 Robert Adam's slick classicism should have been fading into the Greek Revival of the Regency, but not in provincial Bristol. Enter the front door of No. 27 and the rich door and archway surrounds, Ionic capitals with splendidly undercut volutes and fluted pilasters, are nearer in style to the late Baroque of 1730 than to 1792. Comparable town houses in Bath have their grand reception rooms on the first floor. Here in Bristol, William Daniel meant to receive his guests in the ground floor front parlour and dine them in the ground-floor back room. That artisan team had heard vaguely about Adam decoration, but

significantly none of them seems to have been an apprenticed plasterer, so Richard Webb devised a compromise. He carved segmental alcoves with Corinthian capitals and fluted bases as settings for furniture, one in each room, with another pilastered surround to the large window in the back dining room.

An open newel staircase with mahogany handrail and Doric balusters sweeps vertiginously down four storeys, perfect in style for 1792, but the plaster baskets of fruit decorating its lantern are Rococo in spirit and stylistically at least forty years earlier. Webb must have brought in a very old plasterer! Then, in 1793, war broke out, by March Lockier was bankrupt and work stopped in the Square for more than fifteen years. When decorative work began again the front drawing room of No. 27 was given a ceiling rose with palmettes close to the Regency style of John Nash, and a chimney-piece which is just about Greek, but the ceiling cornice is still late eighteenth-century. This atmospheric and miraculously preserved house has been restored by June Burrough as the Pierian Centre, a place for reflection and thought where people can discover their inner strength.

37

Redland Chapel, Redland Green

The Redland Chapel, as John Strahan designed it for the wealthy London grocer John Cossins, who had retired to become the suburban squire of Redland Court, is Baroque theatre with Rococo finishing touches. Try to visit it together with the Royal Fort and Christ Church, Broad Street, all in one Open Doors day, as the three buildings exemplify the rare English Rococo in its first tentative stage, then its rich domestic flowering and finally, at Christ Church, its late lingering into the neo-Classical of the 1790s. Strahan, a Scot, who had designed Redland Court for Cossins in 1735, began the Chapel in 1740, but died in 1741, leaving William Halfpenny to complete the work, adding his own charmingly brash details, all on a miserly ten guineas. It is not a building to be rushed, either inside or out, being full of subtle, almost subliminal architectural motifs. But first of all take in the entrance façade before walking in to experience how the theatre would have worked.

The west front is grand, blind and saucy, an odd combination. The big pilasters are Vanbrughian as at King's Weston, there is only one small window, but the gadrooned cupola is cheerfully casual like a fashionable hat perched on a dowager. Immediately inside is an octagon for social gatherings and chats, with stairs leading up to the best seats in the gallery. Then comes the nave, lined with attentive, beautifully carved cherubs' heads, but dominated by the towering proscenium arch over the apsidal sanctuary. There, instead of a window, a stucco curtain is being raised by an angelic hand to reveal a painted Glory. The sleekly flattened wooden flower wreaths were carved personally by Thomas Paty.

Look back and, instead of saints' statues, there are J M Rysbrack's busts of John Cossins and his wife Martha. Even the altar is pure theatre, a rich drawing-room side table,

close to a design by Batty Langley, with a golden eagle and two flanking angels that look more like harpies. This is usually covered up by a cloth during services, but chapels like this were primarily preaching boxes, not places where the Sacraments were celebrated. Cossins never bothered the Bishop to come and consecrate the place and it has no dedication to any saint.

Back outside again, it is worth spending the time to walk around to the windowless east end to enjoy Strahan's subtle play of recessed surfaces, a very modest Scottish version of the continental Baroque with its more lively animation of parts. The two blackamoors' heads carved as label stops were probably Halfpenny additions to the design, though Thomas Paty's team who built the Chapel had carved several negroes for the frieze and the internal tympana at the Exchange. Their presence indicates how unworried Bristolians of the time were about the morality of the slave trade on which so much of the city's prosperity depended.

38

George Müller Museum, Cotham Park

Most Bristolians are familiar with Muller Road, which connects Ashley Down with the M32, but I wonder how many know the man after whom it was named? Having lived in Cotham for the past fifteen years I have visited his house only once and that was to vote in the local Council elections. I remember a driveway with well stocked flower borders, a spacious lawn with spreading trees and a delightful conservatory where I filled in my ballot paper. The Museum is housed in one of a series of individually styled early-Victorian villas laid out along Cotham Park. It was built in 1852 with an unassuming exterior which gives no clues to the richness inside. The entrance hall has Siena marble columns with deeply undercut Corinthian capitals and a dazzling floor of brightly coloured Minton tiles. This gives onto a staircase lit by a stunning stained glass window. All the cornices, friezes, doors and door furniture are intact in that gentlemen's club classicism before the Great Exhibition of 1851 created a free-fall of stylistic eclecticism. In the largest reception room there are more columns and a riotous plaster frieze with its original Victorian colouring of subtle blues and pinks. Over the marble chimney-piece there is a bewhiskered framed photograph of the great man himself.

The house was acquired by the George Müller Foundation to continue his philanthropic works. Müller was born in Kroppenstaedt, a Prussian village, in 1805 and converted to Christianity when he was twenty. He came to England in 1829 to train as a missionary and met Henry Craik, a Scotsman, with whom he shared a ministry in Teignmouth. They were both very popular with the Victorian ladies of this Devon resort because of the novelty of their accents. Müller followed Craik to Bristol in 1832 where he preached at the Bethesda Chapel on Great George Street. The Chapel was lost in the blitz, but its site is next to the post box at the junction with South Charlotte Street. The city was in the grip of cholera and many children were left orphaned, destined to spend their lives in the workhouse. So in 1835 Müller decided to set up an Orphan Home. The first was in a Georgian terrace on Wilson Street, just off Portland Square in the St Paul's area. By 1849 he had financed a custom-built Orphan Home on Ashley Down, soon to be followed by four others, all designed by the firm of Foster and Wood. These are the grey Pennant stone buildings overlooking the allotments that in 1958 became the Brunel Technical College and are now famous for episodes of the TV programme *Casualty*.

Müller's wife Mary died in 1870 and in 1872 he married a life-long friend Susannah Sanger. She was an ideal travelling companion and they spent the next twenty years in missionary travel all over the world, visiting forty-two countries. Susannah died in 1894 and her tireless husband in March 1898 at the age of ninety-two.

A fascinating exhibition room at Cotham Park, full of photographs and documents, is devoted to Müller's great philanthropic achievements.

39

The Concrete House, Westbury-on-Trym

With its white reinforced concrete walls, horizontal glazing and flat roof, the Concrete House is Bristol's finest example of International Modernism. It was designed in 1934 by Amyas Connell and was completed in 1936. Connell was a New Zealander who came to London in 1924, where he studied at the Bartlett School of Architecture with his friend, soon to become his partner, Basil Ward. In 1926 Connell won the Rome Scholarship and it was whilst travelling that he became a devotee of Le Corbusier, whose polemical work, *Vers une architecture*, had appeared in 1923. The Concrete House was designed with Corbusier in mind, not only in the form of its 'Dom-ino' construction of slabs supported by posts (pilotis) forming a series of inter-related cubes, but in the use of purpose-built fitted cupboards and industrial-style domestic fittings. Connell's design is truly a functional, *machine à habiter*, and many of the original 1930s details survive.

On the ground floor the light and airy drawing room gives onto a dining room; the next room in the sequence was the nursery. There are two downstairs loos, a kitchen and integral garage for two cars with its own work bench. Upstairs, the first owners, the Gunns, had a bedroom each with a shared bathroom and there were two staff bedrooms, a night nursery and a nanny's room. On the roof there is a sun deck, railed in as if on a ship, and the chimney stack for the coal-fired central heating. The house was state-of-the-art for the 1930s, it even had a sound system which was controlled from the drawing room and could pipe music around the whole house through imput sockets for speakers in each room. The main speaker is next to Mrs Gunn's personalised desk in the drawing room. John Gunn made his money in Imperial Tobacco and, like many patrons of the International Modern style, he was left-wing politically and a member of the Bristol Communist Party.

Unlike most preconceptions about these nautical-styled houses, the original colour scheme on the exterior was not plain white, but a plum red on the metal window frames offset by a yellowy Siena colour on the walls. Inside, the main rooms had green and plum-coloured walls and yellow ceilings. Look out for original globe ceiling lights, brushed steel and Bakelite door handles and chrome electricity sockets and switches. When Alan and Vanessa Stevenson bought the house in 1971 there were over 80 broken window panes, water pouring down the steps and from the roof and the floors, which were made of a pale-coloured, green-flecked industrial composite, were spalling and crumbling. The house was in such a state that they were refused a mortgage by the Bristol & West whose agent called it a 'concrete bunker'. It is only recently that these rare and architecturally avant garde houses have become admired, so it is a real credit to the Stevensons that they appreciated it back in the early 1970s. They have overcome the condensation problems with secondary double glazing behind the Williams metal-framed windows, and the flat roof has been renewed twice in the 70-year life of the house. The box hedge in the front garden is original; to the rear there was an orchard and a grass tennis court.

King's Weston House

Most Bristolians, particularly dog walkers, know the exterior of Sir John Vanbrugh's King's Weston House, built between 1710 and 1722 for Edward Southwell in a daring free-form classicism which historians like to describe as an English Baroque. But Open Doors Day offers an opportunity to see something rather more rare than a free-form classical exterior: a free-form interior, just one surviving Vanbrugh room. His handling of spaces and details was so rugged and individual that later owners usually had their rooms redecorated in a more conventional style; at King's Weston, however, his rough and ready staircase hall retains most of its original detail, like classicism experienced in a nightmare. The best way to understand the house is to make straight for that staircase hall, as it is the oldest of several fine interiors. That means giving the entrance hall with its unusually interesting family portraits only the quickest glimpse. Come back to it later. Its towering, unsubtle proportions are Vanbrughian, but all the decorative detail is from a remodelling of 1763-8 by Robert Mylne for Edward Southwell, Lord de Clifford. As Vanbrugh planned it there were two chimney-pieces with an arch between them and it was possible to walk and see straight through into his staircase hall.

Once in that staircase hall it is easy to see why Mylne closed it off; this is a space for gloomy giants. That dramatic 'hanging' staircase which zig-zags up without any apparent support is not original, but the wall niches with their dark frescoes applied directly onto the plasterwork are of the Vanbrugh period and quite possibly by Sir James Thornhill, who painted the dome of London's St Paul's Cathedral. The subtle golden highlights that flicker around the detail of the grotesque urns are typical of his style. Those dark menacing human figures are evocations, rather than direct copies, of celebrated statues like the Borghese *Gladiator* and the Farnese *Hercules*. Going to bed by candlelight in King's Weston must have been a theatrical experience, with at least one bare breasted woman glowering out from the walls.

Back in the entrance hall the atmosphere is more civilized. The highly competent eighteenth-century artist who painted most of these members of the Southwell family did not sign his work, but that full length of Katherine Watson in a blue and silver dress up on the east wall is better than many Gainsboroughs. Another picture which deserves close attention is Sir Richard Southwell of Woodrising in the row below Katherine. Here an original Tudor portrait of striking character seems to have been enclosed in an eighteenth-century extension. Over the entrance door are plaster hunting horns and bows and arrows with the skull of an enormous Irish elk: the kind of trophy Vanbrugh would have approved. After these two cavernous and memorable spaces the other reception rooms come as an anti-climax, but they deserve to be seen for their Rococo plasterwork ceilings: competent modelling, but nothing like the inspired creativity of the Royal Fort.

41

The RAC Supercentre, Bradley Stoke

Whether it is celebrating the mystery of the Blessed and Indivisible Trinity, as Sir Thomas Tresham's Elizabethan Triangular Lodge at Rushton in Northamptonshire does, or the triune majesty of the RAC, as does Nicholas Grimshaw's 1993 Supercentre at Bradley Stoke, there is something essentially dramatic and unsettling about a three-sided building. With a square or a rectangular structure you know where you are. There is a façade in front of which to pause, but with a triangle there is always the excitement of how the designer is to get back to where he started in the shortest possible time. It makes for an exaggerated three-dimensionalism and the completeness of a great toy.

It is only that slightly toy-like quality about the Supercentre that makes one question whether or not it is Bristol's finest modern building to date. The RAC is always in healthy competition with the AA and they wanted their Supercentre to assert their gleaming, streamlined relevance. Grimshaw has given them a silvery-blue lighthouse, presiding over the junction of two major motorways and, in certain holiday seasons, over two major traffic queues, memorable as an image yet, because of that ingenious three-sidedness, suggesting more the esoteric symbolism of a Renaissance conceit than an angular twenty-first century modernity.

That sense of overt cleverness grows stronger with a visit. What looked to be a three-storey building turns into four storeys, the bottom one lying down on angular pylons in a sunken, the word 'defensive' almost springs to mind, moat, that has to be crossed on a causeway close in design to a drawbridge. The interior is supremely elegant with a disturbing tension on every floor between the upright portions and the boldly sloping outer walls of steel and glass. Again there is this feeling of an applied wit in the unity given to the entire space, all four storeys, by the lilting, tilting ingenuity of the central stairs which rise on cam-shaped – triangular with curved corners – platforms and seem to be hung on, rather than supported by, linking sub-stairs to the open-plan floors. Fabric sheets like sails cover the concrete ceilings diffusing the light, which gives the interior a particularly nautical feel.

Noise and glare are excluded by 718 panes of tinted, double-glazed panels, each one weighing a quarter of a tonne; 290,000 metres of cable support its complex technology. That moat is fragrant with herbs and flowers, even the car-park, triangular again, is planted like an orchard. The boardroom on its towering mast, 215 feet above the interchange, surveys the motorways enquiringly like ET in Speilberg's film of that name. The Supercentre may look like a space ship about to fly heavenwards, but the building is Green, man! When Nicholas Grimshaw is your chosen architect you get the best of both worlds: far out yet organically clean. But did he slyly intend the whole complex to subliminally hint at a giant hub-cap?

42

Compact Power, Kingsweston Lane, Avonmouth

This is a building which does exactly what it says on the tin, or in this case the blue metal shed in which it is housed. Designed by the Alec French Partnership, it is relatively small in light-industrial terms, and it converts waste products into power: Compact Power. What is so extraordinary is that there are almost no toxic gases produced from this process. And, to cap it all, this is a local Bristol company in the forefront of chemical technology, leading the world in recycling waste.

Compact Power is on the outskirts of Avonmouth where, having got down from the Severn Beach train, I found a thriving community amongst the factories and huge bonded warehouses. I saw no sign of the plant, but two friendly electricians, Avonmouth-born and bred, knew where it was and gave me a lift. To get to it you skirt a concrete-walled sewage works and then cross a scarred landscape like a back lot of the film *Mad Max* where wrecked cars lie rusting, rows of abandoned fridges and freezers wait in line for disposal, and a great hulking incinerator, now thankfully disused, lowers threateningly overhead. Cowering behind this once belching behemoth is Compact Power, looking more like a B & Q store or a mini Ikea.

The plant is managed by John Clist who is passionate about waste. Instead of incinerating rubbish Compact Power uses pyrolysis: baking the waste at very high temperatures in a steel tube to convert it to carbon, other inert materials and gases. It passes through a pyrolyser, gasifier, cyclone, oxidiser, bypass damper, boiler and lastly a bag filter. The whole process is explained for Open Doors visitors by a power-point presentation at the plant. At the end of the sequence the materials can then be re-used to produce power. When it is fully operational this small plant will be able to process 8,000 tonnes of waste products every year. So,

for a very small cost of about £2 million, we can say goodbye to unsightly and environmentally unfriendly landfill sites. To handle the rubbish of a large city like Bristol a much larger plant will be needed, but even that will cost only about £20 million, modest indeed when one considers the savings in new sources of energy that are by-products of the process.

The Environment Agency is excited about the prospect of this new, clean technology, and both the Friends of the Earth and Greenpeace have welcomed the initiative. Current tests show that what emissions do escape are way below levels set by the strictest European standards. In future almost all our waste could be handled by these small plants set on the outskirts of cities in trading estates where they will blend in with the other units and, because the process is quiet and there are no plumes of acrid smoke, recycling will go on undetected. As John drove me back to Avonmouth station I saw a heron flapping by the chemical factories and I felt hopeful about our ecological future.

43

The Green House, Hereford Street, Bedminster

An ideal Open Doors day itinerary would be to go straight from the new Bristol & West HQ, in that complex around Temple Square where giant structures in a tired, run-down tradition of steel frames, brick and concrete jostle each other, to the Green House where you should sit down in a living willow seat and think about architecture and how we should be building.

The contrast is as refreshing as a pint of pure cold water; the Green House has grown out of its wooden structure almost as naturally as the Douglas Firs that supplied its timber. Remember that scene in the Harrison Ford thriller, *Witness*, when the Shaker community erect a barn together as a religious co-operative of wooden units and ropes and muscle power? That was roughly how the Green House went up in five months before February 1996: an integration, based on the Segal method, of supporting trunks and beams that you can take in as you enter, a beautiful, satisfying, structural logic. Ceiling, walls and floors are all wood and, just as a classical building has an order on the capitals of its columns, so the Green House has evolved a new order of four big struts bolted together at the top of the pine trunks that hold the roof. Go into the loo and there is a massive column of rough-hewn golden wood shooting up beside the lavatory pan to disappear into the ceiling. Can you get more honest in your building than that?

A lovely informality, functional and unpretentious, runs through the rooms. A kitchen and sink unit share an office with computers and files. The staff, who mostly come to work on bicycles, are as friendly as their environment. The Federation of City Farms and Community Gardens wanted an HQ that exemplified their environmental creed and here in Bedminster, between Kwik Save, a scatter of light industry and the railway embankment, they have got exactly what they asked for: a poem of a building in a wild garden next to a car-park reached through Japanese-style log gates. There are few places in Bristol more hopeful for the future.

Enjoy the wild garden on your way out. It grows affectionately around the dull wooden walls on their tree trunk pilotis. Honeysuckles tangle the verandahs and a series of different spaces illustrate the diversity of small-scale organic methods. Strawberries grow for the picking around the willow seats. Lorry tyres have been turned into plant pots. One glorious grenadier of a globe artichoke was flowering when I was there; apple trees and golden elderberries grow side by side, just asking to be turned into jam, and the irises were flowering in that real rarity, a garden pond that looks as if it has filled a natural hollow from a natural spring. The only slight flaw in the complex was a predictable one. Even these miracle workers have not managed to harmonize the little car-park of golden gravel into the otherwise perfect ecological whole. Cars do not fit.

44

Bishopsworth Manor House, Church Road

This has to be the most generous bargain in the entire Open Doors offering free tours, lasting an hour and a half and conducted by Royston Griffey, the scholarly and infectiously enthusiastic owner of this enchanting small manor house, poised at the very end of the naïve English Baroque.

Bishopsworth Manor was built by the wealthy Smyths of Ashton Court as a home for a daughter who had chosen not to get married, a dower house for a spinster. It dates from 1710-20 when fashions in exterior and interior design were changing and its anonymous local builder was trying to keep up to date while being confined to limited dimensions and working on the site, with existing cellars, of a farmhouse that had probably been in existence already for as many as 600 years.

Before making the tour it is rewarding to spend some time thinking about the composition of the main entrance front. The obvious point is that its designer must have admired Sir John Vanbrugh's strange arcaded chimney-stacks at King's Weston House. He produced a miniature version of them here, creating at the same time a splendid viewing platform up on the leads. Imitation did not go much further, but the bucolic architect had not heard of the latest austere Palladian designs that were becoming current around London. Instead he put together a rather too steep pediment, set pineapple finials on the dormers to match those on the gateposts and placed a flaming urn within the swan-necked broken pediment of the central door-case. That segmental-headed window immediately above it has no relation to the other windows, but the effect is modestly engaging and amateur, a really likeable composition.

The entrance hall is attractively proportioned and full of good furnishings; notice how the rooms on each side would have worked socially. First on the right is the Dining Parlour with a cherub and shell-hooded buffet niche in the wall. On the left are two rooms, Morning Parlour and Drawing Room, which have been thrown into one. Originally they would have been on the same scale as the Dining Parlour. Keep that in mind, for the whole house is a miniature and as a result the proportions of its raised-and-fielded panelling are elongated in comparison with the rooms it contains so handsomely. All the window shutters have survived.

The staircase is the jewel of the house, with perfectly turned alternate Doric and barley-sugar balusters and a ramped dado rail with fluted pilasters. Arguably this elegant feature led up to a reception room on the first floor, but the dressing room opening off from it suggests that out here in the provinces it was used as a master bedroom. There are many more rooms and original features, including an extraordinary Dickensian chimney sweep's view up an eighteenth-century flue, but these should be left as surprises for its fortunate owner to reveal.

BOOKS OF RELATED INTEREST

A Bristol Eye: the city seen from new perspectives Stephen Morris and Tim Mowl
An invitation to look again at many of Bristol's well-known buildings and to seek out others less well known. The diversity of styles is astonishing – from classicism through Victorian eclecticism to Art Nouveau, Art Deco and High-Tech functionalism. £11.99

Bristol Before the Camera: The City in 1820-30 Sheena Stoddard
More than 100 watercolour paintings from the celebrated Braikenridge Collection showing how Bristol looked immediately before the advent of photography. The book includes two of Thomas Rowbotham's remarkable panoramas of the city seen from the surrounding hillsides. £12.99

C20: Bristol's Twentieth-Century Buildings Tony Aldous and John Trelawny-Ross
A look at 100 of Bristol's best modern buildings, from Edwardian arts-and-crafts houses to the RAC's space-age 'Supercentre' on the M4/M5 intersection. £11.99

Sculpture in Bristol Douglas Merritt
Survey of 70 of Bristol's finest public sculpture from Rysbrack's William III, the country's greatest equestrian statue, to contemporary work in and around Millennium Square near the waterfront. £14.99

To Build the Second City: Architects and craftsmen of Georgian Bristol Tim Mowl
A look at the rival merits of Bristol and Bath in which, in his inimitable style, the author shows that Bristol, and in particular Clifton, are the unexplored, undervalued treasure houses of eighteenth-century design. Hardback £19.95

All these books should be available at your local bookshop. If any are not, please ask the staff to order them for you.

IN COURSE OF PREPARATION

The Patys: Makers of Eighteenth Century Bristol Gordon Priest
Public View: A Profile of the Royal West of England Academy ed. John Sansom

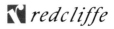